PSYCHIATRIST **DISCOVERS** THE LIFE-CHANGING POWER OF **GOD**

A PSYCHIATRIST **DISCOVERS** THE LIFE-CHANGING POWER OF **GOD**

A Doctor's Biblical Secrets to a New Life
Through a New Way of Thinking

DR. SANJAY JAIN

DESTINY IMAGE™ EUROPE srl
Via Maiella, 1
66020 San Giovanni Teatino (Ch) – Italy

"Changing the world, one book at a time."

This book and all other Destiny Image™ Europe books are available at Christian bookstores and distributors worldwide.

To order products, or for any other correspondence:

DESTINY IMAGE™ EUROPE srl
Via Acquacorrente, 6
65123 - Pescara – Italy
Tel. +39 085 4716623 - Fax: +39 085 9431270
E-mail: info@eurodestinyimage.com

Or reach us on the Internet: www.eurodestinyimage.com

ISBN: 978-88-96727-03-4
For Worldwide Distribution, Printed in Italy.
1 2 3 4 5 6 7 8/14 13 12 11 10

Table of Contents

Why This Book?

Under the inspiration of the Holy Spirit, this book reveals the lies of the enemy that damage your emotions and send you on a roller coaster through life. Practical strategies and techniques are provided to overcome the bondage of negative emotions and battles in your mind. Through this work, I also bridge the gap between psychiatry and Christianity and present valuable insights in a balanced way regarding how your brain, mind, and negative emotions work. I have combined God's gifts of my skills and the expertise of my profession with sound biblical principles.

I know what it is like to battle with negative thoughts that cause distress in your life. I am a psychiatrist and a believing Christian, and I trust Jesus in everything I do and say. I struggled with emotions that were unhealthy for me and for those around me. These emotions caused a great deal of symptoms in my behavior and thinking. I was held prisoner for many years. I tried many methods of finding a solution to the burning issues in my life—even exploring the world of evil via cults, mediums, horoscopes, and religion.

I suffered an intense, emotionally charged upbringing in my early life. My father deserted us and left only my mother to provide protection against all odds. I dived into the ocean of despair, frustration, depression, loneliness, anger, and eventually became suicidal. I finally came face to face with the truth that I found in Jesus in July 1987. I found an overwhelming love and peace in Christ Jesus. He walked with me in every step of my life, and I grew in His holiness and likeness. Although battles were not over, I found the truth, and this truth became my anchor and salvation.

As a psychiatrist, on a daily basis I encounter human suffering as a direct result of negative thinking patterns. However, by no means am I discarding biological, biochemical, or genetic models of mental illness. I have encountered, witnessed, and treated many mental disorders that had and have a biological basis of presentation. However, in an overwhelming majority, these symptoms are due to direct or indirect erroneous thinking. On the other extreme, I have witnessed real cases of demon oppression and possession that have tormented individuals. The psychiatry profession is now recognizing demon possession in its classification system when there is no other explanation to the presentation. However, there is still a big gap between psychiatry, psychology, and Christianity. This gap has created a major stigma, and some churches fail to recognize this due to lack of awareness and their rigid attitude toward mentally ill people.

I start this book with a chapter on suffering in which I have provided an overview of why we go through suffering and why we get trapped into negative emotions, and have highlighted biblical answers. In the next chapter I highlight Jesus' suffering with very explicit information on Jesus' mind-set, His emotional, mental, and physical health from the time of His arrest to the point of His crucifixion and beyond. This chapter is indeed very profound as it certainly deeply impacted me, and made me realize how Jesus suffered intense and emotionally charged trauma, both mentally and physically, and how He overcame these in His thought life. This chapter sets the foundation and scene for our human suffering, our negative emotions, and consequences of these emotions if they are not tamed and brought under control. I have also provided the biological and physical mechanism behind His suffering and death, with explanation of probable causes of death before His final moments. I have explored at some length satan's strategies and his deceptive plans and how he paralyzes a person and prevents you from achieving your full potential.

Finally, I have explored psychiatric disorders, stress-related conditions, and other symptoms that are direct results of negative cognitions. There is a balanced view on scientific and spiritual information with relevant statistics on mental health problems. I have utilized primarily Cognitive Behavior Strategies (CBT) and have combined these with practical strategies from both a biblical and psychological basis in order to overcome negative emotions and battles that are raging in many people's lives today. This also includes practical hints and techniques.

A teacher of psychiatry has observed that the two great commandments of Jesus provide a test of mental health. If a person is able to love God and neighbor, he is mentally healthy. When we see the basic purpose of the church and the nature of mental health in juxtaposition, their interrelationship becomes clear. *To say to a person who is crippled in his ability to love, "What you need is to love God and your neighbor," is like saying to a man clinging to a log in mid-ocean, "What you need is dry land." Nothing could be truer or less helpful.* In working for positive mental health or for the improved treatment of personality problems, the church is implementing its basic purpose by enhancing the ability of persons to love God and neighbor. I see local churches sometimes operating as a polite, middle-class club—comfortable—but irrelevant to human agony.

I am very confident in Christ that this book will influence you in the right direction and set you free from the bondage of sin, negative thoughts, a victim's mentality, strongholds in your mind; then you can claim what is rightfully yours in Jesus—*victory over your emotions.*

Chapter 1

The Battle of Thoughts and Suffering

WHY DO WE SUFFER?

This is a very thorny question. Severe suffering or tragedy often causes people to ask many questions and perhaps the most perplexing question of all is, "Why did God allow this to happen?" And while we won't always be able to discern what reasons God has for any particular suffering or tragedy, the Bible has much to teach us on this subject.

Suffering and pain tell us that something is wrong. When we are born into this world, we don't experience suffering. But as we grow and mature and go through developmental changes, we learn the ways of the society we are living in, and we develop our own mind-set that is more tuned to our needs and things of this world that gives us comfort. Anything that deviates from our mind-set results in experiencing pain.

Do you ever wonder, *Does God really care about me?* Yes, He does. But I battled with that thought for many years, and I know you may also be battling with the same thought. This battle raging in your mind produces a personality in you that becomes deeply ingrained. Therefore, suffering can produce both mental and physical symptoms. Suffering comes in varying degrees from mild to being completely intolerable. The word *pain* is associated with physical pain but it is also connected or synonymous with emotional or mental agony. It is also synonymous with agony, torment, torture, pain, or distress. In my practice, I come across much mental anguish, pain, and distress and this transpires into behavior that produces mental or emotional symptoms. I hear many people say repeatedly, "I'm no good," "I will never get better," "No one cares for me, so I am the way I am," "I'm suffering because of him/her," "My family, husband, or wife is causing my deep pain." Do you identify yourself trapped into these statements or similar statements? Do you sometimes feel that life is not worth living and you would rather be dead than alive? .

To fully comprehend how suffering is produced and manifests itself through our negative cognitions, we need to understand the importance of our mind, the complexity of our brain, and how it dictates our personality, emotions, decision making, judgment, abstract thinking pattern, new learning, memory, and our day-to-day functioning.

YOUR BRAIN

The human brain is the most complex of all organs. The brain is an organ made up of nerve cells, neurons, circuits, etc. The average human brain consists of more than one hundred billion nerve cells. Our nervous system is our body's decision and communication center. This is like our "air traffic control system," and it determines various modalities of our daily functioning including motor and sensory responses as well as in our daily guiding of our emotions, relationships, behavior, and other daily functioning modalities. Nerve impulses to and from the brain travel as fast as 170 miles per hour.

The clinical specialty of *neuropsychology* bridges interest in the biological functioning of neural cells in the brain, spinal cord, and body with the study of psychological disorders. The neuropsychologist uses objective, scientific techniques to link behaviors to underlying normal and abnormal biological (brain) processes. The clinical neuropsychologist studies patterns of abnormal behavior to infer the biological abnormalities that might be producing or contributing to those behaviors. If we presume that the brain is the starting point for why and how we process *all* mental information (not just cognitive, but interpersonal communications, self-concept, emotional reactivity, personality, learned responses, etc.), then in some aspect, all psychology is *neuro*psychology. Neurolinguistics, for example, is the study of how language shapes our self-concepts and our interpersonal communications. Neurodevelopment psychology is the study of how behavioral and mental characteristics change with nervous system growth. Even psychological concepts of dreaming (and dream content), level of attention, and conscious experience are subserved by brain processes.

Numerous medical and psychological studies have suggested a large proportion of visits to the doctor's office are due to *psychological* problems, many the result of acute or chronic stress.

Stress is a normal process we use to appraise and attempt to cope with emotional threats and challenges. Stressors—events and situations—may be blamed for the uncomfortable effects of stress. But the way we perceive stressors determines whether stress is experienced as a panic or a challenge. While normal stress protects the body in times of threat, prolonged stress may potentially damage the body, including the brain. When a stressful situation occurs, the body reacts with an outpouring of hormones (adrenaline, nor epinephrine, and cortisol). These hormones increase heart rate and respiration, send more blood to skeletal muscles, dull pain, stimulate the immune system, and turn sugar and fat into energy.

The stress response is the body and mind's normal mechanism for addressing stressors. In most cases, the response occurs for a limited time to aid the individual in dealing with a specific stress situation. Then the body returns to a normal, non-stressed state.

YOUR MIND

In psychological terms, *mind* collectively refers to the aspects of our intellect and consciousness that are manifested as various combinations of thought, perception, memory, emotion, will, and imagination. It includes all of the brain's conscious processes. *Mind* is a definition that tries to rescue the essence of humanity. The essence of a person arises from the existence of mental functions that permit him or her to think and to perceive, to love and to hate, to learn and to remember, to solve problems, to communicate through speech and writing, to create and to destroy civilizations. These expressions are closely related with brain functioning. Therefore, without the brain, the mind cannot exist, and without the behavioral manifestation, the mind cannot be expressed.

Perceptions, emotions, thoughts, memory, consciousness, and self-consciousness are intimate and subjective entities that are elusive or difficult to grasp or measure. Brain occupies space and time, and the mind or spirit occupying time and being are only individually experienced and therefore unique. The brain is a continually changing organ in its structure as well as its function. Below those grooves and sulci, there is constant flow of information. Therefore the mind is the neural tissue sewn with the threads of time.

There is a constant interaction between various faculties of brain, mind, body, and behavior, and these interactions are essential for balance between emotional, mental, social, spiritual, and behavior that affects our health.

Once we understand the complexity of our thought life and our mind-set, only then will we be able to realize the realities of suffering. Our own thoughts can generate wellness or they can produce suffering, pain, discouragement, suspiciousness, doubts, fear, wonderings, and reasoning. Over many years, numerous psychologists and psychiatrists have tried to unravel the psychology of thought life in a person and how it produces negativity that ultimately leads to mental disorders and stressful reactions. There are millions of people who are or have suffered from mental illness, which in a majority of people is due to the direct impact of our negative thought life. Then, of course, one has to deal with the stigma attached to being diagnosed as having a mental disorder.

Our thinking pattern can get infected similar to a computer virus. No doubt you know that once your computer gets infected with viruses, it produces unexpected and bizarre behavior that causes instability—you may even lose all data stored on your computer, causing its ultimate death. Certainly in these days of technology we have powerful antivirus software to correct the problem.

Think of your mind and the complexities of your control tower—brain—in a similar way. Once you have downloaded negativity, a critical spirit, low self-esteem, jealousy, bitterness, feelings of low self-worth, guilt feelings, self-condemnation thoughts, anger, a quarrelling spirit, hate, envy, laziness, etc., you have commenced a self-destruct mode in your life, and you will ultimately collapse.

NEGATIVITY

Negativity will eat you up slowly, and if you don't do something about it, the ultimate price many pay is committing suicide. In my practice, I have come across many instances where people have committed suicide. According to United Kingdom National Statistics data, in 2008 there were 5706 suicides over the age of 15 years.[1] Suicide remains the most common cause of death in men under the age of 35.[2] In the United States, there were 33,300 suicides reported in 2006—it was the 11th most common cause of death that year.[3]

It is estimated that 450 million people worldwide have mental illness according to according to the World Health Organization (WHO 2001), which is certainly a staggering figure. I am sure that this figure stands at a much higher level now in 2010.

Mixed anxiety and depression are the most common disorder in Britain, with almost 9 percent of people meeting the criterion for diagnosis. Women are more likely to be treated for mental health problems than men. Men are more likely to have alcohol and drug problems than women.[4] More than 70 percent of the prison population has some or the other type of mental disorder. Suicide rates in prison are 15 times higher than general population.[5]

In the United States, the 2006 statistics show that 26,308 males committed suicide, 6,992 females, 5,299 people aged 65 and older, and 4,189 youth between the ages of 15-24 chose to end their lives.[6] These numbers are alarming to say the least.

Are you suffering from emotional bankruptcy? Do you feel so overwhelmed by every situation that you just give up on everything and are unable to fulfill your responsibilities as a father, mother, husband, wife, single person, employee? Our thought life plays a very important role in the way we handle life and circumstances.

PSYCHOLOGY BEHIND OUR THOUGHTS

So how do our minds work? Why are we held captive by our own thinking? How do we look into "triangles of conflict" within others and ourselves? (The triangles of conflict represent the patterning of a person's inner or intra-psychic world. It can be looked at alternately as mind, body, and soul.) Few of us give much attention to our thought life compared to our outward life.

Psychology by definition is a study of the mind and its various processes that produce symptoms. *Clinical psychology* is primarily involved in understanding, studying, and managing distress or emotional dysfunction that causes mental illness and is reflective in its behavior. When we are faced with a difficult situation or a situation that is causing significant mental distress, human beings react in one of the following ways:

1. Mature defense. For example, we reflect a mature defense by meeting needs through service to others and accepting difficulty by focusing on a different activity; or expressing distress in an oblique way—to "see the funny side."

2. Intermediate defense. For example, individuals displaying this defense either display repression through memory lapses or inexplicable naivety, or by reaction formation in which feelings or behavior are diametrically opposed to unacceptable impulses or feelings.

3. Immature defense. For example, this individual would display passive aggression by ineffective expression of anger toward others or directed toward self; projection where individuals attribute unacknowledged feelings to others; becoming a hypochondriac; or some simply act out.

4. Primitive defense. For example, this individual would display distortions of reality that are psychotic or bordering on psychosis. This defense mechanism will eventually change the personality of a person. I have seen cases where a person repeatedly harms himself or herself by cutting and the common reason is to "release pain and suffering by cutting myself."

Many others constantly suffer from *intrusive thoughts* (automatic thoughts) and *dysfunctional beliefs and attitudes* (dysfunctional assumptions). Intrusive thoughts provoke an immediate emotional reaction, usually of anxiety or depression or it could very well be obsessional thoughts that, for example, cause someone to indulge in pornographic activities.

Have you gone through these kinds of intrusive thoughts or images in your mind that you find it difficult to remove? Dysfunctional beliefs and attitudes determine the way in which situations are perceived and interpreted. For example, your wife returns home extremely tired and exhausted from work, and she might be going through her menstrual cycle. Do you make your own assumptions that she is ignoring you, or worse, that she is having an affair? Do you get provoked easily? Do you form reactions and assumptions based on error in your thought life?

Our thought life untamed will eventually produce a psychiatric disorder that has cognitive (the way we think) and behavioral (the way we react on our thinking) components, and these features have to change if the person wants to recover. Our thought center controls our mind, will, and emotions. People routinely go through an avalanche of negative and intrusive thinking patterns.

People who suffer from repeated depressive symptoms will relentlessly exaggerate even small mistakes and think of them as major failures; they catastrophize expecting serious consequences of minor problems; they over-generalize thinking that the bad outcome of one event will be repeated in a similar event in future; and they tend to ignore the positive and dwell on personal shortcomings or on the unfavorable aspects of a situation while overlooking favorable aspects. Sometimes individuals think that everything is hopeless, which may prevent them from attempting even small changes that could accumulate beneficially.

Do you identify with any of the mentioned situations, emotions, or reaction formations? Are you thinking in black and white terms? Are you drawing too-wide conclusions from a single event? Are you blaming yourself for something for which you are not responsible? Are you exaggerating the importance of events? These questions are common in relation to your specific ideas, beliefs, and situations.

Mark Twain wrote, "What a wee little part of person's life are his acts and his words! His real life is led in his head, and known to none but himself. All day long, the mill of his brain is grinding, and his thoughts, not those other things, are his history."[7] Remember that our imaginations can create either a work of art that is beautiful or turn it into horror movie. When our thought life is negative, we are living in a horror movie.

EGO PROBLEM

We need to control our egos as this can feed further into the way we think. The ego traps us and prophesies about our negative future and will always want more. It has to be right all the time, as it judges for us what is right or wrong; ego wants to feel superior and is easily offended. By gaining understanding and rationalizing what is happening in our lives, we can come to see that our ego is not for our highest good. I look at ego as a neurotic task master that is causing our suffering and unhappiness and stealing our peace away from us. Only we can reclaim control over our lives.

SPLIT PERSONALITY

The term *personality* refers to enduring qualities of an individual that are shown in his way of behaving and relating in a wide variety of circumstances. Assessment of personality is important in decisions about etiology, diagnosis, and treatment. In etiology, knowledge of personality helps to explain why certain events are stressful to the individual. In some cases individual personality is so ingrained due to errors in thought life that it causes the individual to suffer, or causes suffering to other people.

For example, an abnormally sensitive and gloomy personality causes suffering for the individual, and an emotionally cold and aggressive personality causes suffering for others. However, I do not want to elaborate more on personalities but to highlight *split personality or multiple personality disorder*, which is the term used in International Classification of Disease 10 (ICD). This is when two personalities routinely take control of an individual with different sets of behaviors. This is typical of many people as they try to hide their true self from others and expose themselves in unruly behavior. This causes a great deal of distress to the individual and occurs as a result of an error in thinking and relating. What we think determines the course of our actions, and our actions determine our relationships, and our relationships determine our future.

QUESTIONS TO ASK YOURSELF

➤ Do you worry and fret about what tomorrow will bring?

➤ Do you relive and regret what happened yesterday?

➤ Do you stew and simmer in your own juices because *so and so* doesn't treat you better or because life just isn't fair?

➤ Are your thoughts consumed by feelings of not being good enough?

➤ Do your thoughts center around how you want more money, a bigger house, a newer car...

➤ Do you spend the majority of your day beating yourself up—saying you are overweight, old, underweight, klutzy, cursed, etc.?

We human beings have been gifted with the ability to enjoy the company of positive character building thoughts or our thoughts can spiral us downward. Continuing to be negative and ego-driven keeps us on a journey of constant suffering and deep pain.

GOD'S PERSPECTIVE

If God is all loving and powerful, then why does He allow suffering and pain? Religions such as Hinduism, Buddhism, New Age, and Christian Science tend to blur the difference between good and evil— but not the Bible. The Bible says we are responsible beings and when we choose evil instead of good, selfishness instead of love, willfulness instead of God, then we, and others suffers the consequences (see Rom. 5:19). We are the members of a fallen and corrupted race, and though still capable of much good, we somehow spoil whatever we put our hand to. Russian author Alexander Solzhenitsyn, who experienced human nature in the raw in the labor camps of Siberia, said:

> If only there were evil people somewhere insidiously committing evil deeds, and it were necessary only to separate them from the rest of us and destroy them. But the line dividing good and evil cuts through the heart of every human being.[8]

So why do bad things happen, and why isn't the world a better place? There is an answer and it is found in the Bible. But it's not the answer that most people want to hear. The world is the way it is because it's the world that we, in a sense, have asked for. Remember the story of Adam and Eve? They ate the forbidden fruit. That fruit was the idea that there's something more important in life than God Himself. For Adam and Eve, this entailed the hope that they could become like God, without God. They consumed the notion that there was something more valuable in existence than God Himself.

Their story is the story of you and me, isn't it? We have become more self-reliant and self-dependent rather than being dependent on God. This explains that the world we live in isn't a God-intended system. God told Adam and Eve that such a system will be "Cursed is the ground because of you; through painful toil you will eat of it all the days of your life. By the sweat of your brow you will eat your food until you return to the ground, since from it you were taken; for dust you are and to the dust you will return" (Gen. 3:17,19). So life is pain, and difficult and horrible things happen to people all the time. We work to survive or live on state benefits and ultimately die—no one can escape the harsh reality of death. This particular verse from Bible is one of the most profound verses and had a great impact on my thinking as a scientific person.

However, God has a completely different system in mind—one He is fully in charge of, one in which His will is done all the time. After all, who sees every rape, every car accident, every hungry person, every cancer victim, and every abandoned child? God sees all of this and more, all of the time. He is much more upset about the condition of this world than we are, or ever could be. We couldn't handle the amount of pain that God Himself constantly endures. And yet He allows this world to go on—but only for a time.

Next we will explore the causes behind our suffering and discover from these causes how interconnected our thought life is with suffering.

ENDNOTES

1. Owen Bowcott, "Suicide Rates are Going Up"; http://www.guardian.co.uk/news/datablog/2010/jan/28/suicide-rates-data-ons#data; accessed April 27, 2010.

2. www.netdoctor.co.uk and www.medicinenet.com; accessed May 13, 2010.

3. Centers for Disease Control and Prevention; http://www.cdc.gov/nchs/fastats/suicide.htm; accessed April 27, 2010.

4. *Better or Worse: A Longitudinal Study of the Mental Health of Adults in Great Britain, National Statistics,* 2003.

5. Social Exclusion Unit (2004), Psychiatric morbidity among prisoners in England and Wales (1998).

6. American Association of Suicidology, "USA Suicide: 2006 Official Final Data," http://www.suicidology.org/c/document_library/get_file?folderId=228&name=DLFE-142.pdf; accessed April 27, 2010.

7. http://www.cdmedia.co.uk/assets/printables/twain.htm; accessed April 27, 2010.

8. http://www.goodreads.com; accessed April 27, 2010.

Chapter 2

You Can Overcome Suffering

This chapter identifies ten reasons why we suffer, explores the dimensions of each, and presents ways to overcome.

Suffering is the direct result of: our thinking pattern; our foolishness; someone else being at fault; natural disasters; walking in the flesh; holding on to past clutter; the enemy; inappropriate use of the tongue; financial bondage; and anger.

1. SUFFERING IS THE DIRECT RESULT OF OUR THINKING PATTERN

Our future, relationships, lifestyle, success, and failures in this life are all dependent on our thought life. The images in the hallways of the imaginations of our minds are put there by what we think. It is very easy to blame other people, or ultimately God, for the way we are and for failing to examine our own futile thought life that may very well be contributing to our problems and suffering. When in pain, we twist or manipulate truth in our mind and are eager to blame others.

As a result of chronic errors in the way we think and perceive events in this life, we automatically create a "victim mentality." A victim mentality is when you blame everyone else for what happens in your life. People trapped by a victim mentality find it very difficult to move forward in life and become completely paralyzed in their thoughts. It is very difficult to accept responsibility for their own actions and they remain on a treadmill of blaming others who in turn become more powerful in controlling their life.

You suffer repeated assaults in your mind by believing what it's saying to you and you remain imprisoned in destructive thinking patterns. You have created a fortress of blame, negativism, being critical, low self-esteem, low confidence, and you are now in an uphill struggle to get out of the fortress. It may seem that you are on the battlefield in a war and you are repeatedly being assaulted and hit by bullets from your enemy. Even though you have all the weapons to fight and win the battle, you are not using the weapons constructively.

Remember that bad things happen to people all the time; that's how this life is, and you are not immune to it. I am sorry to say that there is no effective vaccination to immunize you from experiencing bad things in life. When you are surrounded by various problems, don't believe in the problems more than the alternatives. Continual negative self-talk affects your behavior, mood, and happiness. So don't base your decisions on wrong assumptions and wrong opinions and views about self, others, and the future.

A person with a victim mentality easily misinterprets what others are saying. If people are being offensive or critical toward you, then perhaps they may have a problem in their own mind and thoughts and that's why they are treating you badly. But at the same time, if you have a negative mentality, you will take onboard everything the other person is saying to you and become a victim in your own mentality.

People with a victim mentality and junkyard thinking focus on faults, blame others, find excuses, create own obstacles, wait for things to happen, hold unforgiveness against others, and are short distance runners who burn out quickly. They feel powerless to bring about change in their lives and very often say, "Why do bad things always happen to me?" They have a hard time making decisions, taking responsibility, and taking action, and they are just confined to a boxed thinking pattern.

There are people who are genuine victims of crimes or perhaps injustices, but what I am saying here is that our response and reaction to any circumstances, events, and people are what define us. I believe that even in the midst of tormenting situations, we have the power to choose our response. I responded by saying no to my ways of thinking and victim mentality, and as soon as I stepped out of the confinements of my boxed thinking, I could see the problems more clearly. However, if you are adamant about leading a victim lifestyle, about allowing other people or circumstances to pilot your future, then you are still traveling down the wrong path of your own choice.

Remember that what you put in must come out. For example, if you put garbage in your mind, garbage will come out; put anger in and anger will come out; resentment in and resentment will be the outcome. No one else has access to our minds or hearts except us, and we are accountable for all that we do and say.

2. Suffering Is the Direct Result of Our Foolishness

Sometimes we do certain things and take certain actions that are by any rational means wrong. As a direct impact of these actions and behaviors, we go through serious sufferings—and in some cases eventual death. If you drive dangerously, disobey the speed limits, and suffer a collision, you may either be physically disabled due to multiple traumatic injuries or even die as result. How devastating this action is on family life and other relationships.

Despite health warnings, some people continue to abuse illicit drugs and alcohol, thus causing damage to their physical health and increasing their chances of being arrested for the crime and incarceration. I have seen and treated people with acute psychosis as a direct result of drug and alcohol usage. I have carried out Mental Health Act assessments on people due to their increased risk of safety. Unfortunately, their mind-set and the way they have structured their thinking will cause them to stumble again.

People who suffer from diabetes, high cholesterol, heart disease, and those who are clinically obese need to carefully bring modifications to their lifestyle. Failure to modify will result in unnecessary health problems.

We create our home environment, and what goes on inside our four walls either negatively or positively impacts every member of the family, particularly children. Children feed on their parents behavior, and they learn and grow to be either responsible or completely irresponsible and unruly children. While I was working as a registrar in Bermuda in child psychiatry, I was overwhelmed by the distressing behavior some children displayed. To engage the family in their overall management posed greater difficulties. As a parent myself, I feel responsible for my children to learn and grow in a positive mind-set. Parents who sit in front of the television and ignore their child's needs will produce a child who grows up to be lazy and sits in front of the television. Parents who argue and quarrel all the time will produce fear in their children and that fear can eventually transpire into severe mental illness, or they may vent their anger in school or against society. Parents abusing alcohol and drugs in front of their children on a regular basis, or parents using profane and filthy language, contribute to raising a generation of children with similar behavior causing a ripple effect over future generations. Let's change that kind of lifestyle!

3. SUFFERING IS THE DIRECT RESULT OF BEING SOMEONE ELSE'S FAULT

Sometimes suffering is brought upon by the actions of another or others. Victims of rape who suffer constant torment and flashbacks of the horrific nature of the incident; victims of war who, during the line of duty, are severely wounded or perhaps handicapped; victims of a terrorist attack; victims of a car crash due to a drunken driver, getting wrongfully fired from a job due to someone else's fault; and certainly this list goes on endlessly—these type of victims usually suffer very deeply. Perhaps the biggest cause of suffering worldwide, though, is war, which stems from human greed of power, money, and land.

Victims of this sort of suffering may suffer from mental illness or acute stress reaction as their minds and hearts have been fed with fear, anxiety, worry, and not knowing what is in store for them in the future. They suffer deep anguish, pain, agony, and torment. However, they still hold the key for *complete recovery* if they change their mind-sets.

4. SUFFERING IS THE DIRECT RESULT OF NATURAL DISASTERS

We hear frequent breaking news about earthquakes, floods, drought, hurricanes, and tsunamis. When natural disasters strike, many times there is no escape. They strike young and old, rich and poor alike and do not spare anyone in their direct path. The aftereffects of natural disasters impact survivors greatly, and they are haunted by the sheer force and magnitude of the disaster and at the same time suffer the loss of their loved ones and possessions.

The power in nature is awesome. We cannot experience an earthquake, a volcanic eruption, a raging sea, or a hurricane without feeling helpless. We live in a world of cause and effect. We know that we can drown in water or get burned in a fire. The universe is governed by natural laws. When these laws are challenged, we shall not always escape.

5. Suffering Is the Direct Result of Walking in the Flesh

Would you like to live in a world where evil triumphs and virtue fails? Would you like to live in a world where might prevailed over right in the end? Would you like to live in a world where there is going to be a happy ending for the wicked? Would you like to live in a world where there are no rules as to how people ought to live or what standards people ought to observe?

It seems to be part of the spirit of the age that many people today would like to live in a world of that kind—an immoral world. We call it "post-modernism." The idea behind the word *post-modernism* is something like this: you live as you choose and I will live as I choose. If we work in the same office or attend the same school, don't ask me anything about my private life, and I won't ask you anything about yours. If you want to live like the men of Sodom and Gomorrah, that's your business and nobody else's. And if I choose to be a thief, adulterer, murderer, rapist, bank robber—that's my business and you should leave that to me.

When we think that God has moved away from us, it is us who have moved away from Him. We live in a society that exerts its influence on us by various enticing means. I have heard many people say, "Life is too short, so just enjoy it while you can!" Certainly we can enjoy life, but how do we do that without harming ourselves or others? Enjoyment or pleasure is something everyone looks for. We are constantly influenced by the corrupt, immoral world around us trying to define pleasure for us. Many people are addicted to pornography. We are constantly living on desires of our flesh that are perishable, which ultimately produces mental warfare that many people find difficult to escape. We are defeated in our minds. Mental warfare is the arena of our thought life.

Because of one man, Adam, sin entered the world and hence the human race came under its dominion. Emil Brunner writes in *Dogmatics*, "Sin is the desire for the autonomy of man; therefore, in the last resort, it is the denial of God and self-deification; it is getting rid of the Lord God, and the proclamation of self-sovereignty."[1]

Then where does sin originate if not in our behavior? In Mark 7:20-23 Jesus says: "What comes out of a man is what makes him 'unclean.' For from within, out of men's hearts, come evil thoughts, sexual immorality, theft, murder, adultery, greed, malice, deceit, lewdness, envy, slander, arrogance and folly. All these evils come from inside and make a man 'unclean.'"

Sin isn't something most people talk about very much. Many churches don't talk much about it either. But the Bible tells us that everyone has sinned, and that every sin earns us the death penalty (see Rom. 3:23; 6:23).

Many people have to deal with all sorts of corruption in this world and unfortunately they become part and parcel of this system. We hear of drug crime, prostitution, pornography, satanism, occult practices, lying, and much more. We live in a rebellious society. We become proud as opposed to being humble.

Are you perhaps living in bondage of: stealing, lying, fighting, quarrelling, anger outbursts, jealousy, lusting, critical spirit, swearing, greediness, laziness, gossiping, gambling, cheating, or controlling others? When these ways become habits, they intrude upon your mind, and if you cultivate them, you create a mind-set and they become a standard for your life. If you continue to live according to these standards, then surely the time will come when you will be reaping the rotten fruit it produces. This will affect your relationships and future, and will largely be dominated by corrupt thoughts. As the Bible says, a person "reaps what he sows" (see Gal. 6:7).

Another very important area of our mind battle is *unforgiveness*. We need to forgive others in order to be free from our past and to prevent the devil from taking advantage of us. Sometimes forgiveness is difficult because it pulls against our concept of justice. Many feel the pain of interpersonal conflicts and the bitter seeds it plants in our lives. But we need to acknowledge these problems before it's too late. Don't wait to forgive until you feel like forgiving because you may never get there.

A "nocturnal invasion" is an attack of the flesh that comes at night, especially when you're asleep or in that half-awake state between sleep and being fully aware of what's going on. During this time, our defenses are naturally low, and fear and sexual temptation often find some measure of success. Night invasion can range from sexual fantasies, physical self-gratification, to fear of an assailant breaking into the house—some will completely paralyze you. When we repeatedly sin, we eventually fall into a sin-confession cycle of bondage. But remember, when sin abounds, grace abounds much more.

Some people are careful not to engage in immoral activities, but yet poison their minds with angry thoughts, negative thoughts, self-pity, and self-condemnation. Therefore, we make choices to either walk in the flesh or in God. The flesh births sins and much more, leading to disruption in your life and putting chains on your thinking. We need to reprogram our hard drives—our brains—and delete any malware, spyware, or virus that can infect us and make us crash and die.

6. SUFFERING IS THE DIRECT RESULT OF HOLDING ON TO PAST CLUTTER

You cannot claim victory by doing nothing about your mind-set. Your mind will tell you various things and constantly remind you about your failures and your wrongs. It will also tell you that you can't overcome the mess you may be in. Many times I meet people who are struggling because of their past. Images from the past continually haunt them and they become confined to past events. You cannot move forward unless you have dealt with your past failures.

What is *spiritual clutter*? It is the inability to nurture and support your purpose in life, which prevents consistent and conscious behavior and decision-making. Spiritual clutter limits your ability to fully develop values and actions that are in sync with your innermost desires.

My definition of spiritual clutter is the cultivation of habits and negative behavior that block out our vision of Jesus. It includes the difficulty or inability to forgive and let go of the past.

We need to be free from the past, otherwise our present and future remains very dim. Are you still collecting emotions upon emotions from your past failures and issues? Do you have any of the problems in the following list?

> Are you still struggling with adultery, sexual addictions, pornography? Even though you are trying to get out of this trap, are you constantly failing?

> Are you still going through the aftermath of rocky relationship? Did your marriage end in divorce because your husband or wife has been unfaithful to you? Are you still harboring bitterness and revenge?

> Are you still dealing with major disappointments in your past life? Do you feel trapped within a circle of disappointments and now you are fearful on embarking on anything new or taking the right step? Are you still holding someone in your life who has always disappointed and saddened you?

> Did you suffer abuse? Are you still suffering from the aftermath of physical or sexual abuse?

> Did you have several broken relationships? Are you fearful of embarking on a new relationship because your mind-set is fearful of breaking down again?

> Are you still dealing with some sin in your life and finding it difficult to break free?

> Have you been wounded so badly in your past that you cannot get rid of the outcomes of the wounds inflicted such as self-condemnation, inability to trust others, socially isolating yourself, or being fearful of displaying love again? Do you have a misconception about God and His existence? Are you unassertive and suffering from low self-esteem? Do you have a deep sense of desperation and depression, addiction to alcohol and illicit drugs, or have ongoing suicidal tendencies?

Do you feel that the way you have become is due to the direct consequences listed? These strongholds in your mind-set are continuously working in the background to keep you in bondage. Webster's dictionary defines *stronghold* as a place dominated by particular characteristics. If you have identified yourself with these characteristics, remember that you have the power to change and dump the rubbish and junk from your past and move forward. Sometimes you may feel abandoned and think that God does not love you, but pause for a moment—I want to remind you that although God can be silent sometimes, this does not mean that He has forgotten you. He has certainly given us a free will and most importantly common sense to start rebuilding our lives. Jesus has given you and me that freedom in the storm; and because of *His* suffering, we are made complete.

Do not recycle your junk—recycling brings the same junk back into your life in a new suit. Get rid of it, burn it down. Deal with the root cause of the problem and not just the symptoms. If I see someone feeling depressed, I will certainly treat the symptoms of depression, but at the same time I will deal with the root cause of that symptom by referring the patient to counseling service.

Therefore, the very first thing you really need to do is acknowledge that you have a problem and issues from your past that are holding you back from fulfilling your destiny and purpose in life. Your life is slow and overwhelmed due to the stickiness of your past. Your mind keeps taking you back to when you suffered deep trauma, hurt, wounds, death of loved ones, etc. These memories make life seem like you are carrying a heavy item up the stairs, which slows your climb. On the contrary, if you climb stairs without carrying anything heavy, you go up much faster. The same principle applies in your thought life that originates from the past but stings deeply in your present and makes your future uncertain.

Write down every self-discriminatory thought you are experiencing and that models your current lifestyle in a negative way. You will be very much surprised that you are indeed carrying pain, guilt, and shame. First and foremost, unload your burdens upon Jesus as He loves you and wants you to experience His peace and love. Remember, He has already dealt with your clutter and sin by His crucifixion and has given you the undeserved victory.

As mentioned previously, you need to forgive others. If you continue to harbor grudges, revenge, and unforgiveness, your spiritual, mental, and emotional growth and health will impeded. Forgiveness is about much more than just saying, "I'm sorry," and acting like the offense never happened. Forgiveness is about mending broken relationships. It's about healing unhealthy relationships. It's about reconciliation and redemption and restoration and renewal. Your ego will tell you that there is no need to forgive, but you know in your heart that you need to move on with life. How can you possibly move on with life if the kettle of your emotions is continuously whistling? You need to unplug the kettle and move on.

Remember those precious words of our Lord Jesus from the cross, "Father, forgive them." Very often I have seen many say the Lord's Prayer, "forgive us our trespasses as we forgive those who trespass against us" but do they really take those words seriously?

Holding on so tightly to not forgiving or letting go of the past affects you and your emotions and has negative consequences on those around you. For example, your children will see that their mother or father is not forgiving, and therefore this will become reality for them—that not forgiving others is good. You don't want to sow the seed of bitterness in your children's lives. Remember, the curse of bitterness produces outbursts of pent-up emotions, grieves the Holy Spirit, causes you to make foolish decisions, causes you to see bad in every situation, and you will continually misunderstand people's motives. If you can't deal with bitterness, bitterness will deal with you. Therefore, you need to forgive others and leave everything behind that is slowing you down. You have lot of potential that you may be unaware of and it is about time that you excel in your God-given potentials and gifting. When you fully accept God's forgiveness, you become a new creation in Christ Jesus. And when you sin again and turn to Him with a repentant heart, you are instantly forgiven and He throws it into the sea of forgetfulness.

Get yourself active and involved in social life and fellowship with other Christians as they can act as a buffer to provide you with the support you may need. Make sure you have an opportunity to ventilate your emotions to someone you can confide in. Ventilating emotions and rationalizing and will put order in your chaotic thought life and will heal your wounds.

Don't just focus on symptoms—deal with the root of the problem. You need to deal with your own disobedience that may be holding you back from fulfilling your role in the present. Remember that devil is a liar, and he will do anything in his power to derail you and paint dim colors in your life of guilt and shame. If you have already dealt with sin in your life, then it's probably the devil still trying to remind you that you really have not changed. You need to receive healing from any unfortunate circumstances that are still keeping you under the dominion of darkness.

Steps to Deal With Past Clutter and Junk

1. Admit that you are powerless over clutter, that your life has become unmanageable.

2. Firmly believe that a Power greater than yourself can restore your sanity.

3. Decide to turn your will and your life over to the care of God.

4. Search fearlessly and take a moral inventory of yourself.

5. Openly admit to yourself, to God, and perhaps others that you were wrong.

6. Decide that you are ready and willing to let God deal with your character.

7. Humble yourself and ask God to remove any shortcomings.

8. Make a list of all of the people who may have caused harm to you, and release them in forgiveness.

9. Try to make direct amends to such people whenever possible, except if doing so would injure you, them, or others.

10. Continue to take personal inventory, and when you are wrong, promptly admit to it.

11. Pray and seek God's righteousness—this is a mandatory ingredient for you to be set free and to have peace.

Having had a spiritual awakening as the result of these steps, try to carry this message to others, and to practice these principles in all your affairs.

7. SUFFERING IS A DIRECT RESULT OF THE WORK OF THE ENEMY

Before I commenced my personal relationship with God, I always had doubts and was skeptical about the existence of satan or devils. I was quite scientifically minded and always believed that there was no evil. Maybe you are a bit skeptical too. But now my view is that if there is good, then the opposite of good—bad or evil—is also present. I believe that there is a spiritual realm and it consists of both good and evil and that many unexplained psychiatric conditions are caused by evil spirits or demonization.

Obviously in the practice of psychiatry, demon possessions are not given much weight and the views are divided. However, there have been a few interesting research papers published in medical journals that highlight demon possession as a cause of mental suffering. The International Classification of Disease refers to trance and possession disorder, and the Diagnostic and Statistical Manual mentions dissociative identity disorder. There is certainly some degree of acceptance in the scientific world that there is a demon entity and it does affect a certain number of individuals. Trance disorders have been defined as "a temporary loss of both the sense of personal identity and full awareness of the surroundings; in some instances the individual acts as if taken over by another personality, spirit, deity or force." The reference goes on to say that "only trance disorders that are involuntary or unwanted, and which intrude into ordinary activities by occurring outside religious or other culturally accepted situations"[2] should be included here. This obviously throws light into unexplained symptoms that psychiatrists witness in practice. Therefore, contemporary psychiatry has not totally abandoned demonic terminology.

A demon-possessed individual usually exhibits: verbal outbursts, mostly obscene in nature; violent behavior, vulgar behavior; body spasms and contortions; the ability to speak languages never studied; self-mutilation; superhuman abilities such as abnormal strength or an ability to perform behaviors out of the realm of human possibility such as levitation; cessation of normal bodily functions for periods of time; and pronounced revulsion to symbols, places, people, objects, and ceremonies.

Please note that not all mental disorders are due to demon possession. Does the fact that Jesus always used exorcism in cases of mental illness mean that He never encountered cases of organic brain disorder? While Jesus clearly endorsed demon possession as a valid description of mental illness, He was not necessarily implying that it was an exhaustive explanation. Indeed we now know that it is not.

Common names used to describe satan are accuser, adversary, deceiver, devil, father of lies, enemy, liar, serpent, tempter, and thief. The most common strategy used by the devil is deceiving you in your mind. Remember, the native language of the devil is lie. He does not know any other language. This is where he strikes you and me, by planting a lie in your mind. This is how Adam and Eve were deceived. The Bible says in John 8:44, "He was a murderer from the beginning, not holding to the truth, for there is no truth in him. When he lies, he speaks his native language, for he is a liar and the father of lies." Why would satan attack your mind? Your mind is a place where he can plant a lie, and most importantly your mind is part of the image of God where God communicates with you and reveals His will to you. If satan gets you to believe in a lie, then he can begin to extend his workmanship into your life and into different domains of your life.

Satan's Main Objective

The main objective the devil has for you is to make you ignorant and blind you from the truth. He will put an obstacle between you and fully knowing God's will in your life. When he paralyzes you in your mind, he robs you of your happiness, joy, and peace. Most of all he robs you of all the glorious blessings God has planned for your life. After you are trapped by the devil, you become confused about everything. You make wrong decisions, get involved in sinful activities, and build a wrong kind of life.

Satan's target is without a doubt our minds! He may try any avenue, but his ultimate goal is the minds of God's children. This is the part of us that has control over the rest of us, both the body and the spirit. This is the area of our thinking and decision making. Our mind governs our actions and thoughts, so naturally satan wants control so he can govern the whole person. He will no doubt try to influence the other parts of us to get a foothold, but ultimately he is after our minds. Satan's strategies are all aimed at trying to steal, kill, and destroy. Satan and his troops are out to mislead us and to persuade us to believe in something that is not true.

Satan is an inhuman, merciless fiend whose ultimate goal is the destruction of the human race. In Revelation 12:10, the devil is portrayed as the "accuser of our brothers, who accuses them before our God day and night." Satan encourages believers to worry. Worry neutralizes the soul of the believer. He tries to frighten Christians with regard to physical death. One of the first areas satan will attack is your relationship with

God. He will try to get you to believe that God is angry with you and you are being punished for your sin. He will attempt to get you to believe that God does not care for you. Another method he will commonly use is to make you blame others for your adverse situation. He will make you believe that your situation is bigger than God. Never let satan allow you to think that God is somehow incapable of handling your situation. He will bombard you with confusion. He will puzzle your mind and thinking. First Corinthians 14:33 says, "For God is not a God of disorder but of peace...." Satan attempts to change the focus of the believer. Instead of occupation with Christ, satan wants the Christian to be occupied with self (see Col. 3:1; 1 Cor. 1:10-11), things (see Heb. 13:5-6), and people (see Jer. 17:5).

Emotionalism can lead to great distractions for Christians; so satan puts on a big campaign to control people's emotions. While the emotion is a bona fide function of the soul, whenever emotion takes precedence over Bible truth, it leads to distraction. Those who dabble in ecstatic experiences, public or private, are allowing their feelings and emotions to outweigh doctrine. Under circumstances of edification and spiritual growth, emotion is a tremendous generator of happiness. But emotion has no spiritual meaning or connotation; and emotion cannot be used as a criterion of spiritual condition. Satan also promotes heavily in the area of mental attitude sins such as fear, worry, bitterness, desires for revenge, pride, guilt feelings, lack of love, failure to forgive, hatred, mental adultery, and so forth. A believer is neutralized by sin; and *mental attitude sins are behind all sin.* They are the worst category because they are so devastating. As long as mental attitude sin is taking place, the Word of God is being ignored.

When satan cannot deceive you in your mind, he will do everything he can to destroy your physical body. His primary aim by attacking your body is to make you ineffective for God's work. He causes some physical ailment, accident, or any other disaster that destroys your ability to exercise your motor functioning. This results in suffering. We know that God sometimes permits His children to suffer so that He might discipline them. Our heavenly Father loves us so much that He permits us to be rebels, but then He chastens us so we will want to conform to His will. Obviously God wants us to be self-controlled and disciplined so we can lead abundant lives.

The devil will also make you impatient, which can lead to costly mistakes. The devil knows that if he can succeed in making us impatient, then he can certainly lead us to make stupid decisions resulting in complete destruction of our relationships and into various troubles. Too many Christians have an intellectual religion that brings satisfaction only to their minds but never changes their lives. Other people will have emotional religion and they are dependent only on their feelings rather than knowing and discerning in their spirits what is right or wrong. Satan's target is to capture your will and to control it. He can make you completely independent from God's will and cause acute chronic confusion in your mind to deter you from following the right purpose and being self-controlled.

Satan can also target your heart and conscience and accuses you of failures and reminds you that God and no one else will ever love you. It is important to learn how to distinguish between satan's accusation and the Spirit of God's conviction. When satan accuses you of various things, you will suffer from spiritual anorexia. This is how satan actively deceives people, and they live defeated lives. The Bible says, "Our struggle is not against the flesh and blood, but...against the spiritual forces of evil...Therefore put on the full armor of God..." (Eph. 6:12-13).

Therefore, demonic influence can affect various areas of our lives such as physical health, problems with social behavior (some behavioral problems like stealing, drugs and alcohol, violence, promiscuity, and other sexual sins), emotional behavior (like depression, suicidal tendencies, uncontrollable anger), mental behavior (like complete insanity), materialistic behavior (like compulsive gambling, greed of material possession), poverty behavior (like constantly worrying about poor financial circumstances), and spiritual behavior (like atheism, unbelief, witchcraft, occult involvement). All of these are signs of demonic influence, and they can render you ineffective. Recognizing these symptoms and seeking godly counsel leads you to *victory*.

8. SUFFERING IS A RESULT OF INAPPROPRIATE USE OF OUR TONGUE

Suffering is also produced by a simple slip of the tongue and unwholesome talk. Conflict at home is reality, and it is not funny or entertaining as sometimes portrayed by talk and sitcom television shows. Conflict arises by what we say to each other and how we relate to each other. The wrong words or actions can produce a volcanic explosion of words spoken out in a hurtful way. Remember, the words we speak to each other can build— or destroy. If we do not pay attention to what we say to each other, our negative, critical, profane, and character assault conversations will destroy them and ourselves.

All the sins of temper and tongue should be put away—bitterness, wrath, anger, clamor, evil speaking, and malice. Instead, we need to exhibit self-control and discipline. We need to say to ourselves that even if someone criticizes us, we are not going to react. We are not going to be reactional people but self-disciplined and controlled. We must control our anger. Aristotle said, "Anybody can become angry—that is easy; but to be angry with the right person, to the right degree, at the right time, for the right purpose, and in the right way—that is not easy."[3]

We also need to ensure that our speech does not reflect filth such as telling dirty stories, suggestive jokes with sexual content, or all forms of obscenity. Instead, we need to cultivate the practice of expressing thanks to God for all the blessings in our lives. Our tongues can defile our whole personal body, and the corporate Body of Christ. We can corrupt our personalities by using our tongues to slander, abuse, lie, blaspheme, and swear. Christian writer Clovis G. Chappel puts it this way:

> The faultfinder injures himself…The mud slinger cannot engage in his favorite pastime without getting some of the mud that he slings both upon his hands and upon his heart. How often we have come away from such an experience with a sense of defilement! Yet that was not our intention at all. We were vainly hoping that by slinging mud upon other others we might enhance someone's estimate of our own cleanliness. We were foolish enough to believe that we could build ourselves up by tearing another down. We were blind enough to imagine that by putting a stick of dynamite under the house of our neighbor we could strengthen the foundations of our own. But this is never the case. In our efforts to injure others we may succeed, but we always inflict the deeper injury upon ourselves.[4]

Adolph Hitler and Winston Churchill were separated by the English Channel. But the difference between them was greater than that. Both were powerful and influential speakers; however, they did not use their abilities as speakers in the same way. Hitler used the power of his tongue to destroy. Churchill used the power of his tongue to bless.

James chapter 3 gives us such a wonderful account of taming our tongues. He mentions that our tongues are the smallest part of our bodies, but they have the ability to destroy or build. It can be constructive to others or destructive. The choice is ours, to build others up or destroy others with the same tongue. It is some people's habit to use filthy and profane language, and they do not realize they affect those around them.

God gives us simple suggestions to impart blessings, rather than negativity, to others:

- ➤ Give negative emotions to God and ask God to help you rationalize your thinking that can change into your language.

- ➤ Avoid as much conflict as possible by being thoughtful and helpful.

- ➤ Actively listen to the other person, paying more attention to what is being said.

- ➤ Be slow to speak and quick to listen.

Therefore, the use of your tongue should be primarily to build and teach others with respect, honor, and blessings. Do not abuse your tongue as this will produce immense feelings of unwellness in your soul. Your tongue can poison minds and assassinate characters.

We know how easy it is to gossip about others. And often we criticize and downgrade others. Once we have been engaged in this kind of uncontrolled tongue, we will not see the tears, pain, broken hearts, and ruined reputations we may have inflicted.

Pray daily to control your tongue. Don't talk about anyone unfavorably, as love covers multitude of sin (see 1 Pet. 4:8). If you have something against anyone, go to him or her directly and be courageous enough to forgive and ask for forgiveness in love, and pray together (see James 3:18).

9. SUFFERING IS A DIRECT RESULT OF FINANCIAL BONDAGE

Finances are one area in people's lives that can bring a great deal of stress, anxiety, depression, and even suicidal tendencies. We live in a climate of economic uncertainty. People these days love to live a life of luxury by borrowing beyond their means. Major bank and financial institutions are happy when you borrow money at very high interest rates and then you end up paying double or triple the amount borrowed. In addition to mainstream lenders, there are also loan sharks who are operating in our society who charge an extortionate amount of interest. Many lives are ruined due to mounting debts going out of control. More and more people are filing for bankruptcies or entering into voluntary arrangements with their creditors as a way out of their desperate predicament.

Any major life change can cause you to build up debts or worsen existing debts. Major life changes include loss of job, divorce, bereavement, and the onset of any mental or physical illness. Large debt mentally cripples some individuals to such a degree that they opt to end their lives. What a tragic end! People think, "If I don't grab everything now, I'm going to lose it." Salespeople target people's emotional stimulus, most if not all the time. Another reason why the "having it all whether I can afford it or not" mind-set is so prevalent is the tremendous pressure in society to be like everyone else. It is expected and fashionable to have the latest cell phone model, new clothes more often than necessary, dining out or being seen dining in the most popular places several times a week, etc. Advertising creates big impact. A less malicious reason why people go into debt is the ignorance and immaturity of people who don't know how to handle their money and don't ask for guidance.

The most common reason people go into debt is what I call "premature lifestyle enhancement." It's caused by wanting what you haven't earned, and demanding that you have it *now*. People buy fancy, expensive cars for similar reasons. They want to feel important, to demonstrate their superior status. Unfortunately, fancy cars are only symbolic and they represent status, but—like so many luxury items—are often a better indicator of living beyond one's means. Some people want to get rich quick. They justify expenses by future income. Those who've been infected by the "get rich quick" bug often don't stop with a single purchase. After one failed attempt to become wealthy, they are off to the next opportunity.

It's practically a disease. I should know since a lot of my debt was caused by my desire to get rich quick.

Lastly, of all the causes for debt, this one is the most forgivable. Every person will have unexpected expenses crop up in life. But are they really "unexpected"? The fact is, unexpected expenses are actually quite predictable. They will happen. The only unknowns are when and what. You don't know exactly *when* you'll be hit with an out-of-the-ordinary expense, and you don't know *what* the expense will be related to, but having money in your savings account for these type of "surprises" is the best way to be prepared for the inevitable.

People are increasingly becoming jobless and having to rely on state or federal benefits. If you have missed payments on your loan or overdraft, you may be paying a hefty penalty as that's how financial organizations make their profit. And if you remain a nonpayer, your creditor can start legal proceedings against you. A bailiff may knock at your door who is threatening and certainly forceful. Your credit file is your financial history that is kept by major credit reference agencies. Each time you apply for credit, miss payments, default on a payment, or go bust, it's all recorded on your credit file making you unworthy of obtaining future credit.

I find that credit cards and store cards are the major culprits as more and more people every day spend millions with their plastics. Credit cards are a major addiction in our society. Many who reach their credit limit on one card, start using another credit card. This starts an accumulation of huge amounts of debt. Greed and lust certainly play an important part in this destructive behavior rather than self-discipline. It is not uncommon to find people trying to accommodate a Porsche, a custom-built home, and various other fancy and frightfully expensive gizmos in their budget that can at best fit in a second-hand truck. When you don't cut your coat according to your cloth, chances are good that you will end up with credit card debt, and a sizeable one at that.

Mostly, spending habits are formed quite young. Post high school, many students use their credit cards to help compensate education expenses. The expense of books and accommodation can lead to considerable debt. Apart from these reasons, many students overstretch their newfound financial freedom and indulge in bouts of lavish spending. These are reasons enough to run into credit card debts. For many people, initially borrowing on credit seems like an easy solution; however, sooner or later when it starts to paralyze your daily life, relationships, work, and when you start to ignore demand letters from creditors—this is a sure sign that you are heading downhill.

Unfortunately, debts can lead to major mental stress and disorders. It was interesting to read the news in *The Guardian* in 2006 that a bank refused to recognize mental illness. "The banks are getting together on physical disability issues but on mental illness they lag far behind," says Alison Cobb at leading mental health charity Mind.[5]

A study published in 2009 *Psychiatry News* by the American Psychiatric Association highlighted, "Millions of Americans have watched in dismay as their investments have plummeted in value during the country's economic downturn. Unemployment is growing. Countless people are struggling to pay their mortgage while those who can't have lost their homes. And what has now become a global financial crisis is taking its toll on people's mental health, not just on their pocketbooks. The study, headed by Rachel Jenkins, M.D., a professor at the Institute of Psychiatry in London, was based on a nationally representative sample of people living in the United Kingdom—some 8,600 individuals. All were assessed for anxiety and depressive disorders, psychosis, alcohol abuse, and drug abuse. They were also asked detailed questions about their income and debt. Jenkins and her colleagues then looked to see whether there were any links between mental disorders and income or debt."[6]

According to a study done in the United Kingdom that was published online by the Cambridge University Press in 2008, the more debt people have, the more likely they are going to suffer from mental illness. Advances in Psychiatric Treatment in 2007 published an article[7] that reads, "One in four people with mental health problems in Britain report debt or arrears, which is nearly three times the rate among individuals without similar conditions. Although health professionals commonly encounter debt among patients, some report that they lack basic knowledge to effectively intervene and that patient debt is often not acted on until a crisis emerges."

One of many negative aspects of using credit cards instead of cash is that it feels like you're not spending real money. The pleasant feelings you experience when you purchase the item are disconnected from the unpleasant or painful feelings of making the payment when you get the credit card statement. To really get control of your spending and your credit card debt, you need to examine what money means to you. Make an effort to notice how you interact with money and what beliefs and attitudes you have about money. Studies also show that people with low self-esteem engage in more impulse spending and buying things they don't need.

Obviously getting into debt is easy, just keep borrowing; however, getting out of it can be difficult. Despite what anyone thinks, no one is immune to falling into debt no matter how small or how big the debt is. All it takes is one or two wrong decisions and finances can spiral out of control. But I believe that the biggest culprit is the "I want it now" mind-set. How often do you turn on the television and see various enticing holidays, gadgets, clothes, cars, and luxury items advertised with a buy-now, pay-later scheme? Every time.

Financial Bondage?

Financial bondage is an attitude rather than a condition. You think you know the best for yourself financially and you also think that you can cope with the outcomes. I know people who have lot of money and they don't owe any money, yet they are stressed about money. What the Scriptures say about money and material things has been ignored. Being in debt has been accepted as a way of life. Indeed it is—for worldlings—but should not be for followers of Christ. Simplicity of the Christian life, separation from the world, and dependence upon the Lord for our daily bread has been exchanged for the allurements of this world. Ninety-five percent of all counsel that should be given regarding finances today can be condensed into one sentence: "Owe no man any thing, but to love one another" (Rom. 13:8 KJV). We get into bondage due to:

1. Ignorance and pride.

2. Our wrong attitude toward finances and regarding borrowing money. We see in James 3:16, "For where you have envy and selfish ambition, there you find disorder and every evil practice." If you have the attitude that says, "I've got to have this!" or "I truly deserve this!" Watch out! This is not an attitude of godly steward.

3. Poor planning for your future can also lead to bondage. So how do you recognize financial bondage? Certainly it is not a rocket science to judge for yourself that you are in a deep waters and drowning. However, these are the few common symptoms of bondage: *worry*—you constantly worry about your job, your bank account, old age, etc.; *anger*—do you suffer from episodic emotional flare ups directly linked to your financial issues? Or perhaps you get upset and jealous about what others have and you don't? *Greed*—do you just constantly in need of more material possession?

4. Blaming others for your financial problems.

5. Self-indulgence—do you buy things of little or no utility to you?

6. Poor recordkeeping. You don't keep track of your bank balance and keep overspending thinking that the bank manager will increase your overdraft limit.

If you have any of these symptoms, sit down and seriously think about fixing your problem in a godly way.

Here are some ways you can bring your financial affairs in line with God's plan:

➤ Recognize that God created everything and He owns everything.

➤ Realize that you cannot serve two masters. "No one can serve two masters. Either he will hate one and love the other, or he will be devoted to the one and despise the other. You cannot serve both God and money" (Matt. 6:24).

➤ Plan through prayer and biblical counsel. "Buy the truth and do not sell it; get wisdom, discipline and understanding" (Prov. 23:23). "Plans fail for lack of counsel, but with many advisers they succeed" (Prov. 15:22).

➤ Take responsibility. Don't run away from it. Running away from responsibility doesn't make the problem disappear.

➤ Create a budget planner, accurately recording your income and expenditures. Make sure that your expenditures first and foremost cover your mandatory bills like rent, mortgage, utility bills, and taxes.

➤ If after budget planning you find that there are some surplus funds, start repaying your debts. It is better to suffer a bit of hardship than to keep accumulating debts.

➤ If there are no surplus funds left, you need to pick up the phone and speak to your creditors to make temporary arrangements to help you. Creditors look for people who are willing and honest.

➤ Do not ignore reminders you may receive from creditors, and promptly answer letters from your bank or credit card companies.

➤ Be disciplined and do not borrow any more money.

➤ Watch your daily spending and cut down on doing things and buying things you don't need.

➤ Right now, your unconscious limiting beliefs may be keeping you from being financially successful, but as you begin to build up your feelings of self-worth and develop a positive attitude about yourself and about money, you'll attract positive things into your life. As you do so, you'll feel less of a need to generate positive feelings by purchasing things, and you'll find it easier to stop buying items you don't really need.

➤ Recognize that if you are still struggling, seek professional help. There are nonprofit and government organizations willing to help. "Let the wise listen and add to their learning, and let the discerning get guidance" (Prov. 1:5).

➤ Recognize it is wise to save.

➤ Realize that debt impairs your spiritual freedom and causes suffering beyond recognition. "The fruit of the Spirit is love, joy, peace, patience, kindness, goodness, faithfulness, gentleness and self-control. Against such things there is no law" (Gal. 5:22-23).

> ➤ God wants you to be a good steward of money, and tithing is an important part of being set free and obeying His commands.

10. SUFFERING IS THE DIRECT RESULT OF ANGER

The cancer of anger consumes many people's lives. Being able to express ourselves in anger can be good or bad. We all get angry. I have lost my temper many a times. But for some, anger spills over into their daily lives to such an extent that it becomes like a cancer—spreading rapidly and affecting our physical and mental well-being. Chronic and persistent anger can lead to physical health problems of coronary heart disease, hypertension, stroke, and cancer, and generally leads to poor health outcomes. Anger also leads to poor decision-making and impulsive behavior. Psychiatric illness is common in people classified as "problem angry people," and they have high rates of self-harm, suicide, and depressive illness. Sometimes people who remain confined in their anger suits can develop paranoid ideas leading to schizophrenic-type illness. We may get angry due to feeling frustrated, hurt, rejected, and hostile. Anger can expose the real person inside, and if it is not controlled or tamed can lead to disastrous outcomes. Ecclesiastes 7:9 says, "Do not be quickly provoked in your spirit, for anger resides in the lap of fools."

Anger is "an emotional state that varies in intensity from mild irritation to intense fury and rage," according to Charles Spielberger, Ph.D., a psychologist who specializes in the study of anger.[8] Like other emotions, anger is accompanied by physiological and biological changes; when you get angry, your heart rate and blood pressure rise, as do the levels of your energy hormones, adrenaline, and noradrenalin.

Anger can be the result of internal or external events in your life such as having distressing memories of childhood abuse, being a victim of crime or war, loss of loved ones, worrying or brooding over your personal problems, etc. External events that can lead to expression of aggression or violent behavior could include getting stuck in traffic. Some people release their anger while under the effect of alcohol or illicit drugs, and sometimes weekend scenes at bars and clubs become violent clashes that end with fatalities.

When we get angry, our thinking, feelings, behavior, and relationships can be affected, creating a vicious cycle of misery for us and those around us. Anger can also be a response to a perceived threat, resulting in physical, mental, and verbal assaults, difficulty in relationships, and possibly a complete mental breakdown. Mental health problems secondary to anger can have devastating effects on person's social, occupational, and family life. Anger is linked to the "fight, flight, or freeze" model; however, anger is such a strong emotion that it usually always chooses "fight" from the other two options.

Why Do People Get Angry?

Anger is caused by your inability to emotionally and mentally cope with any given threat. If you have chronic and long-standing problems with anger that are ruling your life, then you may have some deep-seated issue that you have been unable to resolve, and your coping and defense mechanisms may be immature or ineffective. For example, some people may opt for consuming excessive amounts of alcohol or engage in uninhibited behavior such as overindulgence in spending or sexual promiscuity. In a research article in the Journal of Social and Clinical Psychology in 2007 on "Understanding Anger Disorders,"[9] S. Mabel highlights following issues on what makes us angry:

> ➤ Interruption of goal-directed behavior when time is important. How many of us find it difficult to control our emotions when you have an objective to complete certain task during the day and there is someone who is constantly causing obstacles for you to achieve your goal of the day?

> ➤ Experiencing personal degradation or unfair treatment and you feel powerless to stop it. There could be a situation at your work where you feel that your employer is being unfair to demote you; however, you are fearful of raising your concerns due to potential of job loss and hence earnings. This causes intense anger inside you and you are just containing this for it to explode one day.

> ➤ Being treated unfairly, unkindly, or in a prejudicial way.

➤ Being the object of dishonesty or broken promises. This can certainly affect our work or married life. There are large number of divorce suits being filed in the courts due to marital unfaithfulness. You feel that you been robbed by the shopkeeper who charged you a very high price for the item that you later discovered was only half the price you paid.

➤ Having one's authority being disregarded by others. Many a times when children disobey their parents, it can cause profound anger in parents. A couple who are constantly quarreling and arguing for the battle of the fittest with different point of views and disrespecting each other.

➤ Being ignored or treated badly by others. This goes without saying that when you are ignored and your feelings and emotions are secondary compared to other person, you feel frustrated and upset. This is typical of "Me First Mentality Syndrome."

➤ Experiencing harm because of one's negligence toward oneself. This can be further explained by an example of a man who constantly abuses his body by smoking and alcohol and unfortunately gets diagnosed with lung cancer. He will constantly blame himself and will get angry with himself. Similarly a person who makes unwise financial decisions that lead to severe financial crisis will start to take his anger out on himself but sometimes these individuals can blame others.

➤ Being the object of verbal or physical assault. This can escalate the situation and causes malignant outcomes. Physical abuse cases do not just happen in clubs or pubs but also behind the closed doors of Mr. and Mrs. Right. Children can witness their parents arguing, verbally swearing at each other, and physically assaulting each other.

➤ Being shown by others' behaviors that they do not care.

➤ Being a "helpless victim."

We need to understand that societal changes are also influencing our emotions and they are also in part contributing to our angrier personality.

We are embracing what is morally unacceptable and rejecting the truth. Our emotion of anger becomes a hallmark of our thought life that produces stinking anger, which spills through constantly into our lives and into those around us. We try to defend our anger and use profane language, when it is our thought life that is hijacking our emotions and converting it into an acceptable form of behavior so that we can be looked at as an object of innocence. Professor Richard Laynard and Oliver James are two influential authors who have examined life in 21st-century Western society. Oliver James stated in *Observer*, 2007, that as a society we are getting angrier. Laynard in his publication *Happiness* states that despite 50 years of economic growth in the UK, we are no happier.

There is a problem of both anger and aggression. Aggression is commonly adopted by the person as a behavioral response to correct the problem that the person perceives to be incorrect. This is a maladaptive form of reaction that can result in physical aggression and thus sometimes culminate into accidental death or homicide. Then there is *rage*. We come across all sorts of rage, from road rage to parking rage, that are associated with modern-day maladaptive behavior with underlying or core problem of anger and aggression. This could be result of a threat to our ego and status, which can produce a catastrophic chain of reaction in our emotions.

The Mental Health Foundation carried out a survey in 2008 of adults over 18 years of age in the United Kingdom with a sample size of 1,974 people. Survey results show that the category "Our experience of anger in ourselves and those around us" revealed that a third of the sample (32 percent) say they have trouble controlling their anger (higher in women and young people). More than one in four (28 percent) stated that they worry about their anger, one in five (20 percent) stated that they ended a relationship or friendship due to anger. The category "Anger in our society" revealed the startling fact that 64 percent of people surveyed believe that our society is getting angrier.[10]

The British publication Sunday *Times magazine*, on July 16, 2006, published the results of a survey showing that: 45 percent regularly lose their temper at the work place; 38 percent of men are unhappy at work; 27 percent of nurses have been attacked at work; there has been a 59 percent increase in air rage; more than 80 percent of drivers have been involved in road rage incidents; 71 percent of Internet users admit net rage; every day 270,000 people take time off work due to stress; 5 million people suffer work-related stress in the UK; 65 percent of people are likely to express their anger over the phone rather than face to face.

This list goes on and on and it appears that anger, aggression, and rage have become deeply ingrained into our lives as much as our pets. We care for them, feed them, nurture them, grow them, mature them, and ultimately they have the potential to be used as a weapon to destroy others and ourselves. What a sad state of affairs!

Biblical Perspectives

Anger turned to bitterness can take on a power all of its own and ruin good people. It can lead to hate—the opposite of love. The person filled with anger often ends up the most damaged not because of what has been done, but because he or she is unwilling to forgive. God makes it very clear that unforgiveness damages both the trespasser and the trespassed. Be careful about harboring resentment!

Jesus Himself instructs us about anger, and His command carries with it a great sense of urgency: "Therefore, if you are offering your gift at the altar and there remember that your brother has something against you; leave your gift there in front of the altar. First go and be reconciled to your brother; then come and offer your gift" (Matt. 5:23).

Paul says in Ephesians: "In your anger do not sin: Do not let the sun go down while you are still angry" (Eph. 4:26).

These two passages instruct Christians to handle anger quickly. We are not to let anger sit and fester, where it will doubtlessly cause greater problems down the road. Taken together with the verse quoted from Ecclesiastes, all three warn us to handle anger very carefully, as anger is frequently inherently destructive.

There are four faces of anger from a biblical point of view that we have discussed earlier. The four faces are: *rage*, wrath is described as a kind of anger that desires revenge; *resentment* describes anger that stems from grievance, an anger that a person suppresses over a long period of time and if continually nurtured will turn into *bitterness*; and finally *indignation*, an anger that rises up in us when we see someone being mistreated or unfairly.

Righteous Anger

Anger is not always bad, and the Bible shows many examples of appropriate anger. See, for example, Psalm 7:11. The "wrath of God" means that God gets angry—we call it righteous anger. Jesus was angry in Mark 3:1-6. He was angry at Pharisees for their selfish motives. Jesus was angry when he saw that the house of the Lord had been turned into a den of thieves (see Mark 11:17). Jesus got angry for the right things. His anger was not directed at a person nor was it selfish in nature. Jesus was not angry because He was targeted or attacked. Jesus was angry when justice was denied. We, too, have to use our anger for the right things. It is good for us to use our anger against the devil and its forces for holding people in bondage and praying with zeal that can deliver many from satan's clutches. Let us learn to direct our anger in a righteous way.

What Can You Do About Anger?

First and foremost as I mentioned previously, you have to recognize and accept responsibility for your anger, and you must be willing to change. Paul says, "Do not let sin reign in your mortal body so that you obey its evil desires" (Rom. 6:12). The only way to bring your anger and your thought life under stricter regulation is by ensuring that you bring every thought under the captivity of Christ. This will be your starting point in dealing with anger. Another important part of dealing with anger is to be willing to engage in the therapeutic process of dealing with strongholds in your mind that are producing harvest of angry emotions in your life.

You need to be self-controlled. This is a powerful fruit of the Holy Spirit. Self-control comes with practice and with more practice, you will mature and grow in controlling the disease of anger. Discipline your thought life and rationalize your thoughts that are producing turbulence toward alternative explanations. Philippians 4:13 says, "I can do all things through Christ who strengthens me" (NKJV). Apply this Scripture to your thought life. Tell yourself that you are not going to be a slave to anger.

Also start dealing with even minor issues as these minor issues can lead you into a cascade of anger and rage. Small issues can quite easily become resentments. Learn to deal with the conflict and try to resolve any crisis by problem-solving. Make sure you do not over generalize a given situation. If you are unsure about a certain thing in your mind, take a step back and do not immediately react.

Also when dealing with anger and another person, it is important to control and restrain your tongue as discussed previously. Solomon says, "A gentle answer turns away wrath, but a harsh word stirs up anger" (Prov. 15:1). Many times people are quick to respond to any given issue or situation and use language that is demoralizing, degrading, obscene, and assassinates character. When you're angry, spreading gossip is hard to resist. But malicious talk is like wildfire; it consumes those who spread it and those who listen to it. Don't display your dirty clothing; keep it in the laundry room. Don't let your anger escalate to the point of doing damage. Don't use your words as a weapon or a control mechanism. It's OK to express your emotions in a healthy way, but keep them in check. Your goal must be to resolve the problem and strengthen the relationship, not "sound off" and wound the other person. You'll need a good strong dose of grace to overcome. Remember, your words can live in the heart and memory of a person and go all the way to the grave with him or her. We say, "Sticks and stones may break my bones, but names will never hurt me," but it's not true. A person can die of a crushed spirit, and the one who spoke the words can live to regret the damage he or she inflicted and never get a chance to undo it.

Find the root cause from which your anger is originating. You must acknowledge these thoughts, rationalize them, and make sure you delete the negative, soul-crushing emotions in your life before they turn into a fully grown problem. Put tighter reigns on your actions as well.

Ensure that you are not entangled into the web of confrontation with someone who only raises your emotional profile. All through the process, your anger must be restrained and controlled. The reason for this, "man's anger does not bring about the righteous life that God desires" (James 1:20). Keep the situation solution-focused. Someone said that fellowship is like two fellows in a ship—one can't sink the other without sinking himself. Since it takes two to tango, acknowledging your own imperfections makes it easier for someone else to acknowledge his or hers.

Set limits, rules, or guidelines for processing or dealing with the issue. If the other person will not work with you, then he or she may not be interested in a healthy relationship or may not be healthy enough to work through the problem to an agreeable resolution. Communicate by listening. You don't have to agree, but you do need to know what you are disagreeing with. Communication isn't the art of convincing others you are right, but of understanding another and helping that person understand you!

Other Strategies

First and foremost if you think you are going to get angry in a given situation, walk away from it. Do some relaxation exercises. You can get plenty of information on relaxation techniques from your physician and local health center. Calm, relaxing music may also soothe you.

Restructure, change your cognitions, the way you think. Remember, when you are angry, your thinking becomes exaggerated and over-dramatic. Logic defeats anger, because anger, even when it's justified, can quickly become irrational. So use cold hard logic on yourself. Remind yourself that the world is not "out to get you," you're just experiencing some of the rough spots of daily life.

Start practicing some simple problem-solving techniques. Find a friend in whom you can trust. It is equally important that you find a friend who is not a slave to anger and is self-controlled. Share your concerns and views and see what logical answers you can come up with together.

You can also certainly seek professional help. Anger management programs must be selected carefully on the recommendation of a psychologist, a qualified counselor, or a physician knowledgeable in the field of anger treatment. While many anger management programs have numerous worthwhile qualities, some programs may not serve to address the issues at the core of an individual's chronic anger. Learn about anger and assertiveness. Read about them and if possible, find an assertiveness training or other personal development group.

ENDNOTES

1. Emil Brunner, *Dogmatics: Christian Doctrine of God* (Cambridge, UK: James Clarke & Co. Ltd., 2003), 92-93.

2. http://splithope.org/dissociative_disorders_ok.html; accessed May 31, 2010.

3. http://www.brainyquote.com/quotes/authors/a/aristotle.html; accessed April 28, 2010.

4. http://articles.christiansunite.com/article11038.shtml; accessed April 28, 2010.

5. Tony Levene, "The illness that banks refuse to recognise: bipolar disorder can leave its victims destitute—yet lenders deny them the support they need," October 28, 2006; http://www.guardian.co.uk/money/2006/oct/28/accounts.saving; accessed May 13, 2010.

6. Joan Arehart-Treichel, "Study Sheds Light on Relationship Between Debt, Mental Illness; *Psychiatric News*, January 2, 2009, Vol. 44, Number 1, page 5; http://pn.psychiatryonline.org/content/44/1/5.2.full?sid=fa5316f7-bc33-4501-871a-6d298893640f; accessed April 28, 2010.

7. Chris Fitch, et. al., "Debt and Mental Health: The Role of Psychiatrists," *Advances in Psychiatric Treatment* (2007) 13: 194-202. doi: 10.1192/apt.bp.106.002527 http://apt.rcpsych.org/cgi/content/abstract/13/3/194; accessed May 13, 2010.

8. "Controling Anger," American Psychological Association; http://www.apa.org/topics/anger/control.aspx; accessed May 13, 2010.

9. Celia Richardson and Ed Halliwell, "Boiling Point: Problem anger and what we can do about it," Mental Health Foundation Report, 2008; http://www.angermanage.co.uk/pdfs/boilingpoint.pdf; accessed May 13, 2010.

10. Ibid.

Chapter 3

Jesus' Suffering—a Medical and Psychiatric Perspective

I begin this chapter with a couple of crucial verses from the Bible as they form the basis of our understanding of the suffering of Jesus. Jesus' sufferings and thought processes shed much insight into our weak human mentality, and hence form the basis of our foundation in overcoming our mind roadblocks—encouraging us to clear the obstructions in our lives. I am not implying that life will be without challenges; however, once we get the foundations placed right in our minds, we will then have the power to overcome.

> *But He was pierced for our transgressions, He was crushed for our iniquities; the punishment that brought us peace was upon Him, and by His wounds we are healed* (Isaiah 53:5).

> *Just as there were many who were appalled at Him—His appearance was so disfigured beyond that of any man and His form marred beyond human likeness* (Isaiah 52:14).

Please pause for a couple of minutes and close your eyes. Journey back in time in your mind to the time of Christ and try to bring your imagination into Jesus' sufferings—both physical and mental. I want you to create a picture in your mind of the cruelty that Jesus went through—not as Son of God but as *you and me*, pure flesh and blood. Just for a couple of minutes I want you to focus on this, and pray that God will give you strength to read from the medical and psychiatrist perspective the gruesome, chilling, nerve-racking, and profoundly horrific description of the Son of God, this Man Jesus.

I am going to describe chilling events that changed the course of history, and I want you to be prepared to read the explicit and gut-twisting chain of events that started from the point of Jesus' arrest all the way to His crucifixion. The word *excruciating* comes from the Latin, excruciatus, or "out of the cross." In every true sense, Jesus' death was that, and so much more. Jews never imagined the Messiah would suffer for the sake of humanity. Power and might, force and charisma, victory and triumph were words associated with the Anointed One. Suffering was not. And yet hundreds of years earlier, the prophet Isaiah had foretold of the Messiah's suffering with astonishing precision. The Messiah would be a "Man of sorrows," One acquainted with grief. He would be a Man despised and rejected by man. He would be wounded for the transgressions of the people and bruised for their iniquities. Through His lacerating stripes, healing would come.

I always tend to look at any medical or psychiatric condition from a scientific and medical-evidence basis. This is a reflection of my training as a doctor; and I also to look at medical conditions and psychiatric diagnosis from biological, biochemical, or genetic point of view. However, when I researched the medical and psychiatric complications that Jesus went through, I was not just in dismay and shock, but tears were non-stop. Each time when I think of Jesus in that sense, my heart grows heavy and I can sense the pain, mental anguish, and trauma He went through during His final hours before His crucifixion and death. Certainly Mel Gibson's blockbuster movie, *The Passion of the Christ*, describes some of Jesus' sufferings. Immediately after its release in cinemas and on video, there was a huge outcry to ban the movie due to the gore, blood, and horror shown in the film. In my opinion, the movie is exceptionally good in depicting the last 12 hours of Jesus Christ's life on earth. It truthfully depicts what is in the Gospels; a minimal few artistic liberties were taken, however, without affecting what is portrayed in the Bible. I sometimes fail to understand the mentality of those who thought that *The Passion of the Christ* should be banned, but find it entertaining to watch bloody horror movies.

As part of my medical training, I performed my clinical work in Emergency Medicine. As you probably know, accident and emergency departments in any hospital are the busiest places in the hospital. I saw many patients suffering from multiple fractures and heavy loss of blood due to traffic accidents, stab and gunshot wounds, patients in cardiac arrest, patients who were seriously burned, who had lost limbs, and many more types of traumatic physical situations. Medical professionals working in busy ERs have to be constantly on adrenaline in order to manage patients appropriately and quickly within set time scales—delays can obviously cause death. These patients are not only suffering physical pain but they are also in deep mental agony. The family or friends who accompany them are also suffering.

We find it difficult to bear the pain of even a minor scratch on our skin. How much more Jesus went through—physical pain, emotional agony, mental trauma—and still He did not utter a mean or angry word all the way until death came upon the cross. Please do not consider me irreverent when I ask if men and women have not faced death with more courage and have not endured extreme physical agonies for longer periods of time than Jesus did. Heroic people have faced death without flinching and have endured torture willingly, as painful as the human body can feel, for days. Even the thieves on either side of Jesus endured longer than He did. The fact that Jesus was bearing our sins would not make physical suffering more intense, because guilt of sin is spiritual rather than of the flesh.

I am going to take you on a journey from the Garden of Gethsemane, through His trial, His scourging and chastisement, and ultimately to the point of death on the cross. I begin with an article written in the Journal of American Medical Association in 1986, which states,

> Jesus of Nazareth underwent Jewish and Roman trials was flogged and was sentenced to death by crucifixion. The scourging produced deep stripe like lacerations and appreciable blood loss and it probably set the stage for hypovolemic shock as evidenced by the fact that Jesus was too weakened to carry the crossbar to Golgotha. At the site of his crucifixion his wrists were nailed to the crossbar and after the crossbar was lifted to the upright post (stipes) His feet were nailed to the stipes. The major pathophysiologic effect of crucifixion was an interference with the normal respirations. Accordingly death resulted primarily from hypovolemic shock and exhaustion asphyxia. Jesus' death was ensured by the thrust of a soldier spear into his side. Modern medical interpretation of the historical evidence indicates that Jesus was dead when taken down from the cross.[1]

In the Garden of Gethsemane

Prior to Jesus' arrest, He was indeed a very healthy and robust man. He led a very physically active life. The rigors of Jesus' ministry would have precluded any major physical illness or weak general constitution. Accordingly, it is reasonably obvious to surmise that Jesus was in good physical health before walking into Gethsemane.

The Garden of Gethsemane is at the foot of the Mount of Olives, within the walled grounds of the Church of all Nations (also known as the Church of the Agony). It's a peaceful garden among a grove of ancient olive trees, looking back at the eastern wall of the City of Jerusalem. The Aramaic word *Gat-Smane* means oil-press, so seems to refer to olive trees planted around the area at that time. Remarkably, the Garden of Gethsemane still contains dozens of ancient olive trees that date to approximately 2,000 years old. The garden is where, according to Christian traditions, Jesus and His disciples retreated to pray after the Last Supper, the night before He was crucified.

So what went terribly wrong here? After Jesus and His disciples celebrated the Passover, they came to the garden. While in the garden, Jesus took His three disciples—Peter, James and John—to a place separated from the other disciples. "Then Jesus went with His disciples to a place called Gethsemane, and He said to them, 'Sit here while I go over there and pray'" (Matt. 26:36). During this time, Jesus was going through emotional distress, a sense of loss, a sense of depression and despair. However despite this, Jesus' cognitions, His behavior, judgment, and perception, were still under His control, and He exhibited a profound degree of mature defense mechanisms. He was also certain in His thought life at this time that these events were prophesied to happen and that He would be fulfilling His Father's will for the good of all humanity. However at the same time, we need to understand that because He was still in flesh like you and me, He suffered emotional contractions and severe distress.

When Jesus went away to pray in solitude, He asked His disciples to stay awake and watch. During His prayer, He experienced an overwhelming burden on His soul as He anticipated becoming a sin offering for us. These moments were ones of severe mental agony as His emotions were laid bleeding in the garden. He called His Father and prayed, "My Father, if it is possible, may this cup be taken from Me. Yet not as I will, but as You will" (Matt. 26:39). This cry to His Father reveals His anguish that was going through His soul, His thoughts. He even told His disciples Peter, James, and John that His soul was exceedingly sorrowful, even to death. Despite His mental torment, emotional bleeding, and deep anguish, He was still prepared to do His Father's will. Did He get the answers to His cry to His Father? There was none; the heavens were silent.

BLOODY SWEAT—FACT OR FICTION

Of the four Gospel writers, only Dr. Luke referred to Jesus' ordeal as "agony" *(agonia)*. "And being in agony He was praying very fervently; and His sweat became like drops of blood, falling down upon the ground" (Luke 22:44 NASB). This was indeed a very interesting and fascinating symptom that Jesus went through while He was under extreme heaviness, mental anguish, and soreness in His soul. I discovered its medical definition as follows, "The excretion of blood or blood pigment in the sweat is called *hemidrosis*. It is a very rare medical symptom when human beings sweat blood and this primarily occurs in the extreme circumstances when someone is subjected to intensity of stress or affliction to an extent that sweat glands in our skin which are supplied by multiple blood vessels and due to rhythmic constriction and dilation of these blood vessels, the blood oozes into the sweat gland which pushes the blood through your skin pores as droplets of blood mixed with sweat."[2]

According to Dr. Frederick Zugibe, Chief Medical Examiner of Rockland County, New York:

> The severe mental anxiety…activated the sympathetic nervous system to invoke the stress-fight or flight reaction to such a degree causing hemorrhage of the vessels supplying the sweat glands into the ducts of the sweat glands and extruding out onto the skin. While hematidrosis has been reported to occur from other rare medical entities, the presence of profound fear accounted for a significant number of reported cases including six cases in men condemned to execution, a case during the London blitz, a case involving a fear of being raped, a fear of a storm while sailing, etc. The effects on the body are that of weakness and mild to moderate dehydration from the severe anxiety and both the blood and sweat loss.[3]

So this made clearer that the medical evidence supporting Jesus symptoms were very real.

PSYCHIATRIC SYMPTOMS

Therefore, from these accounts, it is clear that Jesus, as a human being, suffered just like us. He knew what to expect and was prepared to complete His journey through this time to surrender to His Father's will. Can we imagine His thought life second by second in the Garden of Gethsemane? He went away to pray on three times and on each occasion He had no direct answer to His prayer. He prayed to His Father to take the cup of suffering away from Him. This cup is a reflection of His innermost torment, anxiety, feeling of loss, wave of depression, and also a reflection that He was about to take the sin of the world upon Himself and become sin. He would have also been suffering from insomnia due to severe anxiety and must have been very tired as were His disciples who kept falling asleep. Jesus repeatedly reminded them to watch and pray. What a powerful and beyond-description display of His love for humanity.

Jesus' response at this time from psychiatric point of view is in three parts:

1. The emotional component to His response was predominantly anxiety with autonomic arousal leading to panic, tachycardia (increased heart rate), increased muscle tension, and dry mouth as well as depressive responses, which are generally associated with events posing a loss and anxiety associated with events that pose a threat.

2. Jesus displayed great coping and problem-solving strategies by seeking help from His Father and also making and implementing plans to deal with the situation. He also displayed emotion-reducing strategies by expressing His emotions to His disciples as when He told Peter, James, and John that His soul was exceedingly sorrowful, even to death. He also positively reappraised the whole situation and gave in to His Father's will for Him. Under these sorts of circumstances, many of us will display maladaptive coping mechanisms by using alcohol and drugs, deliberate self-harm, and aggressive behavior that releases feelings of anger.

3. Jesus also displayed mature defense mechanisms by remaining composed in His personality and exhibiting no maladaptive pattern in behavior.

Clearly Jesus presented from the psychological point of view a mixture of anxiety and depressive reactions. This could also be classified into another category of acute stress reaction and acute stress disorder when Jesus suffered anxiety in response to threatening experiences; depression is response to loss that was reflected in Jesus' cries to His Father and there was silence in return. Jesus experienced both anxiety and depression, which possibly occurred together because stressful events often combine danger and loss. At this point Jesus did not have any previous biological, biochemical, or genetic basis for His symptoms. He was enduring them for only one reason—to redeem humankind.

During His final moments in Gethsemane, Jesus was betrayed with a kiss by one of His own disciples. The betrayal of sinless Jesus represents one of the biggest anomalies so prevalent in our society-corrupt heart these days. How would you react if someone you loved very much betrayed you? What would be your emotional reaction to such an experience? Would you forgive the person and move on with your life, or would you suffer with a deep-seated wound filled with a cocktail of emotions ranging from depression, loss of self-esteem, hurt, pain, suicidal feelings, and the urge for revenge?

Jesus' thought life was disciplined and under control despite the fact that He was going to go through gruesome and heart-wrenching trials and punishment, all the way to the cross. Jesus could have summoned twelve legions of angels to assist Him—but that would have only frustrated the divine plan.

JESUS' TRIALS

Jesus' betrayal and arrest are important parts of His passion and so are His trials. During the trials, Jesus' suffering became more humiliating, degrading, and above all physically abusive. How would you feel if you had to go through the court system and face a trial; what sort of emotions would you experience and have to endure? Going through the justice system can have its own challenges and can cause a severe imbalance in your emotional and mental health. Jesus' trials certainly changed the entire course of human history. On one hand Jesus continued in His disturbed mental state; but now He also had to endure the trials, face physical abuse, emotional abuse, verbal abuse, humiliation, insults, and the list goes on.

Then there was the illegal aspects of Jesus' trials that include: Trials could occur only in the regular meeting places of the Sanhedrin (not in the palace of the High Priest). Trials could not occur on the eve of the Sabbath or Feast Days or at night. A guilty sentence could only be pronounced on the day following the trial.

Soon after His arrest, Jesus went through both the Jewish and Roman trial systems. He was taken to Annas followed by Caiaphas. "Having arrested Him, they led Him and brought Him into the high priest's house. But Peter followed Him at a distance" (Luke 22:54 NKJV).

> Now the chief priests, the elders, and all the council sought false testimony against Jesus to put Him to death, but found none. Even though many false witnesses came forward, they found none. But at last two false witnesses came forward and said, "This fellow said, 'I am able to destroy the temple of God and to build it in three days'" (Matthew 26:59-61 NKJV).

Jesus initially refuses to answer any questions posed, but later He pleads guilty claiming that He is the Son of God. The high priest tears His garments upon hearing the confession, judges Jesus with blasphemy, and declares the death penalty. They blindfold Jesus, strike Him on His face with their fists, and spit on Him (see Matt. 26:67-68).

This ruling and subsequent abuse no doubt incited a great deal of further torment in Jesus' mental state and caused a great deal of distress because now this whole chain of events was becoming more scandalous. Then Jesus was brought to trial in front of Pilate, the governor of Judea. When they brought Jesus to him, they did not say He blasphemed but rather said that Jesus self-appointed Himself to be the King who would undermine Roman authority. However, after perhaps lengthy discussions, Pilate could not find any fault in Jesus. Pilate then ordered Jesus to be tried before Herod. Herod's men also treated Jesus with contempt and mocked Him. Similarly, Herod could not find any fault, and sent Jesus back to Pilate for his decision in the matter. Pilate tried to simply chastise Jesus and release Him thereafter.

FLOGGING AND SCOURGING

Then Pilate took Jesus and had him flogged (John 19:1).

A *scourge* (from Italian *scoriada*, from Latin *excoriare* = "to flay" and *corium* = "skin") is a whip or lash, especially a multi-thong type used to inflict severe corporal punishment or self-mortification on the back. *Flagellation* or *flogging* is the act of methodically beating or whipping (Latin *flagellum*, "whip") the human body.[4]

Scourging, practiced by the Romans, was a cruel punishment that usually preceded crucifixion. The only ones exempted from scourging were women, Roman senators, and soldiers except in cases of desertion. Normally there were between one and six trained Roman officers, called lictors, who were responsible for executing the blows to the victim. The lictors chosen to administer blows had some medical training. They knew how to wield the whip so as to open wounds that had already formed. The instrument used for scourging is a short whip called a flagrum or flagellum to which was attached several braided leather thongs of variable lengths. Knots were tied in the ends of each thong, and sheep bone or iron balls were inserted into the knots at the end of each thong. Jewish law allowed forty lashes to the prisoners. The Pharisees, always making sure that the law was strictly kept, insisted that only thirty-nine lashes be given in case an error occurred during counting. (See Deuteronomy 25:3.) The Roman law did not have any set limit on the number of blows that could be executed. The object of the scourging was to bring the victim to near death and weaken him. Many prisoners did not survive this punishment, which was also called "half death." The extent of blood loss may well have determined how long the victim would survive on the cross.

Jesus was tied up to the post, stripped with His back, buttocks, and legs exposed, His face badly bruised, His beard probably ripped off in patches, bloodshot eyes, weak and dehydrated, unable to bear weight on His legs, and still not a word on His lips. The scourging was done by "professional men." The strokes are never one on top of another, but always one after another, approximately at equal distance. Jesus must have been bound in such a way that He was in a rigid, almost immovable position; He could not twist himself around to avoid the blows.

I offered My back to those who beat Me, My cheeks to those who pulled out My beard; I did not hide My face from mocking and spitting (Isaiah 50:6).

The atmosphere surrounding this gruesome punishment shouted with screams of pleasure. The soldiers appear to be in a satanic frenzy, they lash out with the whip full force, again and again across Jesus' shoulders, back, buttocks, and legs. With each stroke of the whip, a painful shudder can be seen as waves of never-ending pain shoot through His body. His back is now a mass of shredded skin, muscle, and deep wounds. (See First Peter 2:24.) Chunks of His flesh were torn from His back to such a deep extent that His ribs were showing.

A crowd gathered, and encouraged the soldiers to continue their sadistic practice; each blow causing more blood loss with arterial bleeding ensuing. Blood pours out non-stop during the violent whipping. Shreds of His skin hang on His back, some is ripped away and attaches to the whip, some shreds of His skin fall to the ground. The smell of blood is profound. Jesus became such an unrecognized mass of torn flesh that it is even difficult to recognize Him.

At this point, Jesus must have been so weak and almost paralyzed that He may have been unable to hold Himself upright—but He was bound by His wrists to the post high up.

Finally, this brutal game is over. Jesus was untied and falls to the ground. After some time, He regained His strength and pushed Himself up considering bruised, battered, raw wounds, profuse bleeding, and excruciating pain. A crown of sharp thorns was shoved into His head, a robe draped over His shoulder, and the Roman soldiers continued to mock Him as He suffered. Next they spat on Jesus and struck Him on His head with a wooden staff. When soldiers tore the robe from His back, His wounds were exposed.

As a flesh and blood human being struggling physically, Jesus' mind and spirit were absolutely resolute and crystal clear because He knew the course of His life—His sacrificial death. Certainly now at this stage, Jesus was very distressed not just only in His mind but also in His physical being. If we look again at the chain of events that took place from the time of His arrest, His trials, and His flogging and scourging, this gives us clear picture of the psychological and medical domains of His symptoms. From the psychological point of view, He went through severe physical abuse, taunting, mocking, shouting, and the whole of hell was breaking loose on Him. Victims of physical and emotional abuse suffer from acute reactions to stress, post traumatic stress disorder (PTSD) symptoms, and anxiety and depressive reactions. Victims of repeated physical assaults develop cognitions of humiliation, shame, and are vulnerable to further attacks. They lose confidence and self-esteem and to these problems are added issues of betrayal that constantly plague a victim's mind. During this course of time, Jesus would have suffered a great deal of anxiety symptoms, including dry mouth, epigastric discomfort, constriction of chest, awareness of missed heart beats, tremors, severe headaches, painful and aching muscles, dizziness, tingling in extremities, and breathlessness.

The effects of experiencing traumatic stress, either as a witness or direct victim, are a major public health problem in many countries worldwide, with consequences of potentially severe psychological, behavioral, medical, and social dysfunction, including PTSD and other anxiety disorders, depression, and psychotic conditions, as well as injury and death. Jesus suffered relentless acts of repeated violence such as being punched, kicked, slapped, whipped, and verbally assaulted.

The physical consequences He suffered were multiple. He also possibly sustained traumatic head or brain injury. The Medical Disability Society Working Party Report on the Management of Traumatic Brain Injury (February 1988) defines Traumatic Brain Injury as: Brain injury caused by trauma to the head (including the effects upon the brain of other possible complications of injury, notably hypoxemia and hypotension, and intracerebral hematoma). In other words, a brain injury is caused at least initially by outside force, but includes the complications that can follow such as damage caused by lack of oxygen and rising pressure and swelling in the brain. When the soldiers put a crown of thorns on Jesus and struck Him on His head, this could have caused brain injury.

A traumatic brain injury can be seen as a chain of events:

➤ The first injury occurs seconds after the accident.

➤ The second injury happens in the minutes and hours afterward, depending on when skilled medical intervention occurs.

➤ A third injury can occur at any time after the first and second injuries, and can cause further complications.

The prognosis varies and depends on the severity of the injury. It is now commonly recognized that even minor head injuries can have long-term consequences (usually psychological or learning disabilities). Serious head injuries can result in anything from full recovery to death or a permanent coma.

Jesus also received facial injuries—his beard was pulled in a frenzied attack, which caused patches of no hair with deep wounds in those areas.

One of the most important aspects of Jesus' physical injuries was His blood loss, which would have initiated a catastrophic chain of events. There are three different types of bleeding episodes:

1. Capillary bleeding is unlikely to be significant unless the wound is very large or there is some abnormality of the clotting system. All but small, shallow clean wounds should be seen by a physician, especially if the bleeding won't stop.

2. Venous bleeding is very similar to capillary bleeding except that bleeding might be quite heavy from a small wound.

3. Arterial bleeding can be very serious. The arteries contain blood under some pressure and in older people in particular this pressure may be elevated and the arteries hardened.

Individuals in excellent physical and cardiovascular shape as Jesus was prior to His arrest and torture, may have more effective compensatory mechanisms before experiencing cardiovascular collapse. These people may look deceptively stable, with minimal derangements in vital signs, while having poor peripheral perfusion (poor skin perfusion with blood flow).

Considering this definition of various types of bleeding, it is apparent that the scourging Jesus suffered produced severe blunt and lacerated trauma and severe hemorrhaging causing destabilization of blood circulation and cardiovascular status.

EFFECTS OF BLOOD LOSS

If blood is lost in sufficient quantity over a relatively short period of time, there are inevitable consequences as was the case with Jesus. These effects:

> ➤ Speeding up of the pulse.

> ➤ Reduction in blood pressure.

> ➤ Dizziness.

> ➤ Cold sweats.

> ➤ Cold, pale peripheries.

> ➤ Gasping for air—"air hunger."

Jesus almost started to slip into hypovolumic shock. Shock is a state of inadequate perfusion, which does not sustain the physiologic needs of organ tissues. Many conditions, including blood loss but also including nonhemorrhagic states such as dehydration, sepsis, impaired auto regulation, and decreased myocardial function, may produce shock or shock-like states. Failure of compensatory mechanisms in hemorrhagic shock can lead to death. An initial peak of mortality occurs within minutes of hemorrhage due to immediate exsanguinations. Another peak occurs after one to several hours due to progressive decompensation. A third peak occurs days to weeks later due to sepsis and organ failure. This was exactly the case with Jesus—His body compensatory mechanisms were active and fighting the severe loss of blood. The mechanisms were functioning extra strenuously.

Jesus' dehydration would have caused significant electrolyte disturbance and His overall clinical features would have included multi-organ system. These would have been, for example, His central nervous system that would have been in altered mental state or acute confusional state; cardiovascular disturbance would have caused tachycardia, hypotension, arrhythmias; renal disturbance would have been evident by oliguria (decreased product of urine) to anuria (non-passage of urine); respiratory system would have been on a high drive with slow progression to perhaps respiratory failure; and He would have also suffered hematological and metabolic disturbances.

CRUCIFIXION

Wanting to satisfy the crowd, Pilate released Barabbas to them. He had Jesus flogged, and handed Him over to be crucified (Mark 15:15).

Crucifixion is an ancient method of death where the condemned is tied or nailed to large wooden cross, of various shapes, and is left on the cross until dead. Crucifixion originated initially in Persia; however, the Romans mastered the technique. The practice of crucifixion was indeed a gruesome, slow, and painful death that took place primarily in public.

Jesus, who was already in severe and excruciating pain both physically and mentally, carried the crossbeam (patibulum) on His shoulders thus exposing deep wounds that were causing intense pain, burning, and more blood leakage due to the direct impact of the heavy crossbeam, which weighed approximately 75-125 pounds. The three synoptic Gospels record Simon of Cyrene bearing the crossbeam.

The place of execution was just outside the city walls. The path from the flogging post to the place of execution is called the Via Dolorosa (Latin for the Way of Grief or the Way of Suffering). In spite of Jesus' efforts to walk erect, the weight of the heavy wooden beam, together with the shock produced by copious loss of blood, was too much. He stumbled and fell. When He fell to the ground face down, He must have sustained additional injuries including to His chest, thus possibly causing cardiac injury. The rough wood of the crossbeam was inflicting more pain into His open wounds. He tried to rise, but His human muscles were pushed beyond endurance.

At the place of execution, the victim was usually given a bitter drink to act as mild analgesia. There Jesus was thrown on the ground with His arms outstretched on the patibulum to be nailed at the wrists between the two arm bones to bear the weight of His body. Nails were wrought iron of 7-8 inches long and when they are hammered into the wrist there is damage to nerves and blood vessels. Wrist joints are a complex structure of bones, ligaments, blood vessels, and nerves. All these in one way or another were injured by the penetrating iron wrought nails into His wrist. As Jesus sagged down on the cross, He put more weight on the nails and excruciating pain would have shot up from His fingers to His arms with an explosion of this severe pain in His brain. Jesus' arms were possibly so stretched in order to get the right position to hammer the nails that most likely His shoulder joints would have been dislocated.

After Jesus was secured on the crossbeam, the soldiers lifted him onto the vertical bar, or stipes. Once in position, they nailed Jesus' feet possibly on top of each other. To achieve this, soldiers would have made some "anatomical adjustments" to his lower limbs in order for the nail to stay in place. If Jesus pushed Himself upward on the cross, He would have had to push against His feet, causing excruciating pain.

After Jesus was nailed into position on the cross, it was raised while the crowd shouted and screamed. With every breath, Jesus experienced excruciating pain. A great wave of cramps set in and He was unable to push Himself upward. As He hung there, His arms, pectoral muscles, and the large muscles of His chest were paralyzed and His intercostals muscles that connect the rib cage were not functioning to aid with respirations. The main pathophysiologic effect of crucifixion is marked difficulties with respirations. He was able to inhale air into His lungs but unable to exhale. Finally, carbon dioxide levels increased in His lungs and in His blood stream and cramps subsided a little bit. Now He is going through possible respiratory paralysis and His heart is struggling to pump blood to maintain oxygenation—He was going into cardiac failure.

Jesus' side was pierced, and out came blood and water. This phenomenon could have been caused by pleural effusion or cardiac rupture/effusion. Normally, a heart contains 20 milliliters of pericardial fluid. When a person dies of a ruptured heart, there are more than 500 milliliters of pericardial fluid, and it would be released in the form of a fluid and clotted blood.

JESUS' LAST WORDS FROM THE CROSS

Spasmodically, Jesus would exhale and take in some oxygen. During these times He uttered these words:

1. Looking down at the Roman soldiers, "Father, forgive them" (Luke 23:34).

2. To the thief hanging beside Him, "Today, you will be with Me in paradise" (Luke 23:43).

3. Looking at His mother, "Woman, behold your son," and, "Behold, your mother" (John 19:26-27).

4. From Psalm 22 He said, "My God, My God, why have You forsaken Me" (Mark 15:34).

5. Jesus gasped His fifth cry, "I thirst" (John 19:28 KJV).

6. Then He started to feel the chill of death creeping slowly and this realization caused Him to say, "It is finished" (John 19:30).

7. With His last breath, He gasped, "Father, into Your hands I commit My Spirit" (Luke 23:46).

CAUSE OF DEATH

From the biblical account of events and in my opinion, it is reasonable to assume that Jesus died as a result of multiple factors interacting and playing vital roles in causing multi-organ failure, asphyxia, dehydration, cardio-respiratory collapse, cardiac failure, and shock. A fatal cardiac arrhythmia would have accounted for the final event in His body shutdown. Arrhythmias are serious, life-threatening emergencies and require urgent intervention to control the heart rhythm by means of active resuscitation and perhaps by using a defibrillator. Sadly, Jesus suffered a severe degree of arrhythmia and most likely ventricular fibrillation that resulted in the fatal shutdown of His system. However, let us briefly look at each possible mechanism of Jesus' death:

Asphyxia: Asphyxia means that the body is deprived of oxygen while there is accumulation of excess carbon dioxide. However, prior to Jesus' death, His body must have reached a critical level of low oxygen-high carbon dioxide levels. Jesus had severe blows to His back and He fell down on His chest, which would have contributed to chest compression and would have been one of the causes of asphyxia. Another possible explanation: the intensity of physical trauma Jesus endured on His body and face would have caused bleeding in His oral cavity and perhaps this would have obstructed His airways, swelling His airway lining, making Him gag. Furthermore, the severe degree of exhaustion Jesus endured would have initiated the process of oxygen bleed and less oxygen going to His brain and organs. All of His body organs are now working in overdrive.

Common signs that Jesus probably displayed were face congestion, facial swelling, and cyanosis due to less oxygen, and He most likely also had some petechial hemorrhages in the skin and eyes. Therefore from the account of Jesus' torture and punishment, it appears that He suffered a great degree of asphyxia.

Dehydration: Dehydration is another factor that played a key role in Jesus' death. We know that up to 75 percent of our body weight is due to water. Jesus, during His final hours was sweating blood and not drinking, thus He suffered severe water loss causing dehydration. He also probably developed a fever causing dry mouth, muscle cramps, nausea, palpitations, and light-headedness. With severe dehydration, confusion and weakness occurs as the brain and other body organs receive less blood. Finally, coma and organ failure will occur if dehydration remains untreated.

Cardiac failure: Heart failure ensued when Jesus' heart was no longer pumping enough blood to His body. As a direct result of Jesus' cardiac failure, He displayed symptoms of shortness of breath, coughing, feet swelling, fatigue, weakness, faintness, His neck veins were probably sticking out, and swelling of the liver. This could have further led to significant heart enlargement and pulmonary congestion. Due to continued dehydration, associated heart failure and other factors that would have caused overload of the cardiovascular system, Jesus would have had pulmonary embolism. Jesus' blood pressure would have been very high and I wonder if He went through accelerated hypertension with symptoms of headache, blurring vision, and renal impairment which would have caused excessive fatigue, nausea, vomiting, and hiccups.

Neurologically: Jesus would have suffered a great deal of impact on His neurological status. The primary factor could have been decreased oxygen to the brain, metabolic and toxic factors that would have impaired His cerebral functions and possible cerebral vascular catastrophes. This would have caused fluctuation in His cognitions and He probably would have displayed signs and symptoms of an acute confusional state. Jesus, at this point, probably displayed some neurological deficits.

Respiratory System: Jesus' thoracic cage would have been impacted greatly during His physical torture. There is a possibility that any foreign body in His mouth may have slipped back into the airway and may have contributed to obstruction. Jesus possibly suffered "spontaneous pneumothorax" caused when there is leakage of air from the lungs into the pleural cavity spontaneously and without any preceding trauma. This can occur in healthy people usually between 20-40 years of age. Obviously Jesus' symptoms of acute respiratory distress with intense breathlessness, cyanosis, perspiration, and shock, would have indicated that Jesus, at the time of crucifixion and also during the whipping, suffered tension pneumothorax. This would have slowly led to acute respiratory failure. Severe hypoxia would have severely affected His central nervous and cardiovascular systems, which are entirely dependent for normal functioning on constant and adequate oxygen supply. This would lead to varying degrees of anxiety, restlessness, some degree of agitation and mental confusion. Increased accumulation of carbon dioxide would have caused Jesus to have bounding pulse, a flushed face, and warm, sweating hands. In addition to this, Jesus would have suffered dilation of cerebral vessels producing headaches, restlessness, muscle twitching, and flapping tremors. Another symptom is abdominal pain. All this would have led to respiratory distress syndrome, which is a serious complication that can develop during the course of a number of clinical disorders.

Acute heat reactions: During Jesus' trials and punishment, He would have suffered severe cramps that are painful spasms of the voluntary muscles and are attributable directly to high environmental temperature, relative humidity being of little importance. This would have progressed to heat exhaustion; and in the early stages the symptoms include headache, vertigo, nausea, vomiting, apathy, fatigue, and weakness.

PHENOMENA DURING AND AFTER HIS DEATH

Darkness fell and there was an eclipse. The sky was darkened, "for three hours" (see Luke 23:44). The Gospels state that the veil of the temple was torn from top to bottom (see Luke 23:45; Mark 15:38). The Gospel of Matthew states that there were earthquakes and splitting of rocks. These supernatural phenomena occurred at the time Jesus died.

Survival on the cross usually lasted from a few hours to a few days and was inversely related to the degree of scourging. Jesus was crucified along with two other thieves. One of the thieves was critical of Jesus, but the other thief requested Jesus to remember him. This is quite significant in the sense that despite the sheer intensity of mental and physical anguish, Jesus was still able to show that He was still in control of His thoughts. He told the thief, "Today you will be with Me in paradise." His love did not stop because of what they did to Him. He asked His Father in Heaven, "Father, forgive them because they don't know what they are doing" (see Luke 23:34). What an awesome display of being composed, resolute, and still focused on others—Jesus, full of love and continually pleading for us.

Can we love our enemies like that? Can we forgive others and hold no negativity against them? Jesus, despite His torment and unbearable agony and pain, despite people who accused Him, mocked Him, and caused grave physical injuries, remained ready to forgive and love them. We can do the same if we have the Holy Spirit living within us and lean on Him for strength and power, mercy and grace.

VICTORY!

Victory over death was fully manifested when Jesus rose on the third day and appeared to many people including His disciples. The resurrection is a public testimony of Christ's release from His undertaking as surety, evidence of the Father's acceptance of His work of redemption. There is victory over death and the grave for all of His followers. Jesus rose up in victory. He proved beyond any shadow of doubt that He overcame not just our sins but also our thought life. I see many Christians leading defeated lives even though they know the truth of being set free from every bondage, guilt, sin, and shame. If Jesus lives in us, there should be no room for leading a miserable, guilt-ridden, and shameful lifestyle. In everything we should be able to lead victorious lives as His grace is sufficient for us in our weakness. Victory is not going to manifest fully if we continually believe in our egos, our own mind-sets and lifestyles, what others say or do, if we are continually holding on the thread of revenge, if we continually have a me-first mentality, and most importantly, if we are still firmly believing the lies of the enemy.

Therefore, I believe that the death of Jesus was a direct result of possible cardio-respiratory arrest with heart failure and other indirect factors that would have caused the complete collapse of His organ system with varying degrees of biochemical, hematological, and other abnormalities.

However psychiatrically, although He suffered a great deal of anxiety and depressive symptoms along with hard impact on His cognitions, Jesus was able to keep His thought life under His control and did not harbor bitterness or revenge in His heart. The most remarkable feature of His thought life during this time was that instead of being filled with physical pain and the harsh realities of how people were insulting and physically abusing Him, He was filled with compassion and love for others. He continued to speak with the utmost authority, passion, and love as He was about to fulfill the prophecy and His Father's will for Him. He started the love revolution.

As darkness fell upon Him, all the pain of the world was upon Him, all the rotten sin of this entire world laid upon Him. He took upon Himself our thoughts, lives, guilt, shame, and every fleshly work we ever did or will ever do, and He pleaded for forgiveness for us. He showed all of humankind the power of His undying love.

ENDNOTES

1. William D. Edwards, MD, Wesley J. Gabel, MDiv., Floyd E. Hosmer, MS, AMI; "On the Physical Death of Jesus Christ," *JAMA*, March 21, 1986; 255(11): 1455-1463; http://jama.ama-assn.org/cgi/content/abstract /255/11/1455; accessed April 28, 2010.

2. Jane Manonukul, M.D., et. al., "Hematidrosis: A Pathologic Process or Stigmata. A Case Report With Comprehensive Histopathologic and Immunoperoxidase Studies," http://journals.lww.com/amjdermatopathology/Abstract/2008/04000/Hematidrosis__A_Pathologic_Process_or_Stigmata__A.8.aspx; accessed May 13, 2010.

3. http://www.bionity.com/lexikon/e/Hematidrosis/; accessed April 28, 2010.

4. Duncan Heaster, "The Death of the Cross," http://www.aletheiacollege.net/cross/1-1-4-1flogging__scourging.htm; accessed May 13, 2010.

Chapter 4

Consequences of a Negative Mind-set

In this chapter, I provide you with an overview of what your thought life does to your mental and emotional well-being. I will briefly describe mental health problems that can arise as a direct result of a negative and distorted mind-set. This is important as it helps you understand mental health problems and perhaps will help to reduce the stigma attached to these types of problems.

However, I am not going to write a whole book on psychiatric conditions. It is a very sad state of affairs that every day there are large numbers of people being treated for mental disorders and equally there are people being detained as their mental disorder has reached a nature and degree that they pose a risk to themselves or to others. Worldwide there are millions of people who see mental health professionals for their illness. But this represents only the tip of the iceberg, as many people suffer in silence. The massive Global Burden of Disease study, conducted by the World Health Organization (WHO), the World Bank, and Harvard University, measured the leading causes of disability (counting lost years of healthy life). In developed countries, the ten leading causes of lost years of healthy life from ages 15-44 were: 1) major depressive disorder; 2) alcohol use; 3) traffic accidents; 4) schizophrenia; 5) self-inflicted injuries; 6) bipolar disorder; 7) drug use; 8) obsessive-compulsive disorders; 9) osteoarthritis; 10) violence.

HOW COMMON ARE MENTAL HEALTH PROBLEMS?

Mental health involves how we feel, think, behave, and react on the thoughts going through our minds. It also means how you process information in your mind. One in four people will have mental health problems at some point in their lives, which can grossly affect many areas of their lives including their work, relationships, and finances.

Although the following information primarily addresses the United Kingdom (UK) and Europe, of which I am professionally familiar, the statistics are alarmingly comparable for all developed countries.[1] About 300 people per 1,000 suffer from mental health problems in the UK. More than 4,300 people die by suicide each year in the UK and many more suicide attempts are made. Worldwide, on average about 800,000 people commit suicide every year, 86 percent of them in low- and middle-income countries. More than half of the people who kill themselves are aged between 15 and 44. The highest suicide rates are found among men in Eastern European countries. A study looking at figures for attempted suicides from several European countries, including the UK, suggests that the figures might be higher—possibly as many as 2 percent of people who have attempted suicide will kill themselves within a year of the previous attempt. A British study found that women who have a history of deliberate self-harm (including overdose) are 15 times more likely to die by suicide compared with other women. The risk is particularly high during the six months following deliberate self-harm. The likelihood of a person dying by suicide depends on several factors; mental and physical illness, social problems particularly family stress, separation and divorce, ease of access as a means to complete suicide.

According to a WHO working group, there is ample evidence that social conditions liable to change (such as the constant risk of losing one's job) are among the determinants of suicide. Recent research has shown that divorce is also a major determinant for suicide and particularly common in men.[2] A number of studies have shown that 90 percent of people who die by suicide had one or more psychiatric disorder. The new figures reveal that the impact of mental distress is worsening among some groups. The rate of common mental disorders, typically depression and anxiety, has risen by a fifth among middle-aged women since 1993. Similarly, the rate of self-harm has risen by 80 percent. Mental illness health costs the UK economy £80 billion pounds a year with a population of about 62 million. In the United States, the cost for treating mental illness in 2006 was about $58 billion for a population of about 300 million.[3]

According to WHO, about half of mental disorders begin before the age of 14. Around 20 percent of the world's children and adolescents are estimated to have mental disorders or problems, with similar types of disorders being reported across cultures. War and other major disasters have a large impact on mental health and psychosocial well-being. Rates of mental disorder tend to double after emergencies. Stigma about mental disorders and discrimination against patients and families prevent people from seeking mental health care. In South Africa, a public survey showed that most people thought mental illnesses were related to either stress or a lack of willpower rather than to medical disorders. Contrary to expectations, levels of stigma were higher in urban areas and among people with higher levels of education. By 2020 depression alone will be the second biggest ailment in the world after heart disease, according to the World Health Organization (WHO).[4]

Unemployed people are four times more likely to experience severe mental-health issues, including depression, than people with jobs, according to a survey released in 2009 by the National Alliance on Mental Illness and Mental Health America.[5]

CAUSES FROM A PSYCHIATRIC PERSPECTIVE

The complexity in which psychiatrists or any other mental health professionals operate is vast. I have to remind myself about the complexity of causes and its classification, the concept of stress and psychological reaction. Causes of any mental disorder can be further complicated due to a number of other reasons; for example, causes can be remote in time from the effects they produce. This can be illustrated by childhood problems of abuse or rape that can manifest many years later in adult life. Second, even a single cause can produce several symptoms or behavior. For example, if a child is deprived of parental bonding, this can predispose the child to anti-social behavior, depressive illness, suicide, and other severe behavioral problems. On the other hand, a single symptom can be caused by several different mechanisms. For example, depression in an individual could be the result of several factors, which include genetics, adverse childhood experiences, and stressful dynamics of adult life.

There are several factors that can cause or at least contribute to unstable emotional affairs. These factors are predisposing, precipitating, maintaining:

Predisposing Factors

These factors tend to operate earlier on in a person's life and will dictate your symptoms. These could be genetic, physical, psychological, and social factors in earlier childhood. We all have core attributes and these core attributes will determine our mental and physical makeup. Our mental and physical profiles tend to change as we progress through life and are usually influenced largely by various social and psychological influences. Our personality is modified and changed according to influences, and we develop stronger personalities as a result of our acceptance of a particular idea. This becomes truth for us even though it may not be acceptable to societal norms. Some people will develop an anxious personality, and they will be fearful of certain situations and places, and they constantly worry. Others think that the world is not on their side and these people develop a paranoid-type personality. Our personalities will predispose us to many types of mental illnesses.

Precipitating Factors

Precipitating factors are perhaps are more visible and they tend to cause the effect in you. Again they may be physical, psychological, and social. Physical factors include any illnesses and or drug effects. However for the purpose of this chapter, I will be primarily focusing on psychological and social factors that color your thinking. These precipitants include loss of job, divorce, accidents, financial crisis, etc. When you receive bad news or perceive a threat, you will process that particular information in your mind to decide how to best deal with the given situation. Many people are able to deal with the problem with a minor degree of acute stress reaction; however, others can't. They have tuned their thinking to a frequency of negativism, destruction, and futility.

Maintaining Factors

These factors could be destabilizing the person by provoking demoralization and withdrawal from social activities, which in turn ignite further the person's original mental disorder. These will be further associated with low self-esteem, poor judgment, poor decision-making, low levels of confidence, dependent personalities, and the stigma that comes along with it. Do you feel trapped in situations and dilemmas where you find it difficult to break through?

WHAT IS STRESS?

I hear people use the word stress quite commonly in their daily vocabulary. They associate stress even with non-stressful situations or objects. *Stress* is the term applied to events or situations that may have adverse effects, and these adverse effects could affect you psychologically or physiologically. The factors that produce or induce adverse effects are *stressors*. Everyone is in constant interaction with our surroundings and this interaction creates a dynamics of balance or imbalance. When there is imbalance, we get psychologically distressed. Therefore, when you are under a stress attack, you form a behavioral response to its effects. These reactions could include a rise in blood pressure, activation of adrenaline and nor adrenaline, and the feeling of being keyed-up.

Because of the overabundance of stress in our modern lives, we usually think of stress as a negative experience, but from a biological point of view, stress can be a neutral, negative, or positive experience. Excess stress can manifest itself in a variety of emotional, behavioral, and even physical symptoms, and the symptoms of stress vary enormously among different individuals. Common symptoms experienced by people are sleep disturbance, muscle tension, headache, gastrointestinal disturbance, sexual problems, abdominal pain, heartburn, and fatigue. Emotional and behavior disturbances can cause anxiety, mood changes, and disturbance in eating habits. They may display emotional symptoms of: being in a bad mood, upset, angry, impatient, crying spells, irritability, tension, and hopelessness. Behavior displays include rushing around constantly, starting tasks and not finishing them, unable to concentrate, shouting, and waking up too early in the morning. There may also be greater tendency to engage in excess alcohol and drug intake, cigarette smoking, and poor nutritional choices.

Stress becomes a problem because of the way you process information, which determines the outcome of your psychological and physical health.

Psychology and Understanding Mental Disorders

Psychology is the scientific study of people, mind, and behavior and has contributed significantly in understanding conflicts in psyche, which can contribute to any mental or emotional disorder. People try to make sense of their environment and scrutinize the behavior of other human beings, and this allows some degree of prediction and control.

Modern psychology was brought to the forefront by Sigmund Freud in the late 19th century. Freud certainly wasn't a godly man. He was obsessed with sex and linked every problem of man to the sexual drive. Freud had serious problems.

To a large extent, psychiatric symptoms can be interpreted in terms of radicalized temperaments and extreme emotions. Also, psychology studies have looked into information processing and how errors are made in processing either part or the whole of the information at hand. How human beings interpret situations as positive or negative, dangerous or safe, and so on, is often dependent on attention, memory, and judgment, and this creates a cascade of reaction formation in our minds that forms the basis of inferences about any given situation. Each person has his or her own schemas and belief system, and any deviation from that will cause an effect in information processing.

One of the most interesting concepts in psychological development is psychosocial development. One of the greatest contributors in the development of personality, which I find is intertwined with our thinking, is Erik Erikson's stages of psychosocial development. Erik Erikson studied psychoanalysis and made significant contributions in the study of personality development. He states, "Hope is both the earliest and the most indispensable virtue inherent in the state of being alive. If life is to be sustained hope must remain, even where confidence is wounded, trust impaired."[6]

Erikson also made significant contribution into the concept of identity crisis, and his theories continue to be influential today in our understanding of personality development. One of the main elements of Erikson's psychosocial stage theory is the development of *ego identity*. Ego identity is the conscious sense of self that we develop through social interaction. According to Erikson, our ego identity is constantly changing due to new experience and information we acquire in our daily interactions with others. Each stage in Erikson's theory is concerned with becoming competent in an area of life. If the stage is handled well, the person will feel a sense of mastery, which he sometimes refers to as *ego strength or ego quality.*[7] If the stage is managed poorly, the person will emerge with a sense of inadequacy. In brief, Erikson describes eight stages of psychosocial development as follows:

Infancy (birth to 18 months): This is the most fundamental stage of life when there is trust or mistrust. At this stage, an infant is fully dependent on his or her caregiver and trust is based on the dependability and quality of the caregiver. If at this stage the child develops a strong bond of trust, it results in confidence as the child grows up. However if the care giving is inconsistent or emotionally unavailable, the result will be fear and a belief that the world is inconsistent.

Early Childhood (2-3 years of age): There is a greater sense of personal control at this stage. Learning to control one's bodily functions leads to a feeling of control and a sense of independence. Children who go through this stage successfully will feel adequate and in control, but those who fail will have a sense of inadequacy and self-doubt.

Preschool (early childhood 3-5 years of age): This stage, successfully managed, leads to either taking initiative or feelings of guilt. Children at this stage exert their power and control by directing play and social interaction.

School Age (6-11 years of age): At this stage, through social interaction, children will develop a sense of pride in their accomplishments and their abilities. Children who are encouraged and commended by their parents and teachers develop a feeling of competence. On the other hand, children who don't receive these encouragements will doubt their competence.

Adolescence (12-18 years of age): This is the stage of developing self-identity versus role confusion. Those who remain unsure of their beliefs and desires will feel insecure and confused about themselves and the future.

Young Adulthood (19-40 years of age): This is when development of intimacy or isolation takes place when people enter into personal relationships. Erikson believed that it is vital at this stage to develop strong, close relationships with others that generate a sense of security and, to some degree, dependence. Those with a poor sense of self will develop less committed relationships and will most likely suffer emotional isolation, loneliness, and depression.

Middle Adulthood (40-65 years of age): During this time, people continue to build their lives, focusing on career and family. Those who pass through this stage develop a sense of pride and achievement that they have contributed positively to their community and family. Those who fail at this stage, due to any reason, will feel rejected, inadequate, unproductive, and uninvolved.

Maturity (65 years to death): This stage is primarily focused on reflecting on past life achievements and failures. Some will be bitter and in despair, and others will have a sense of fulfillment even when confronting death.

These theories throw light on our personal development. However, there are many critics to the theories of Erik Erikson. Many questions have been raised referring to Erikson's belief of identity formation. What about those adults who rediscover themselves and develop a different understanding of their lives due to life changes and experiences? Is it possible for an individual to change throughout life? Other theories on development lean toward the individual having psychological development completed at much earlier ages.

CHRISTIANITY AND PSYCHOLOGY

Christianity and psychology have some things in common. They both state that our behavior is the product and process of our thought life. But in describing what those processes are and how to change them, Christianity and psychology take the opposite approach. However in this day and age, in order to understand the human emotions, psychology and

Christianity are indeed to a degree getting bit closer. There are organizations like the Christian Association for Psychological Studies that are trying to fill the gap between Christian beliefs and psychology. The integration of psychology and Christianity is important due to the interface between thought processes and the symptoms it produces, which can help our understanding of human personality.

I find very disturbing that many pastors and church leaders disregard this relationship; and unfortunately, many pastors and leaders lead very isolated and lonely lives due to their ignorance. God certainly wants us to be better equipped for the emotional, spiritual, intellectual, and mind warfare that befalls men and women in church leadership positions. *The Journal of Psychology and Christianity* highlights important topics interconnected with both psychology and Christianity and applying the principles of both produces profound results. One of the articles focuses on this important question, "Is forgiveness a necessity or a nicety for the Christian?"[8] A close examination of Matthew 18:15-35 reveals that this question is vital for everyone concerned with the psychotherapeutic and counseling fields.

> *"If your brother sins against you, go and show him his fault, just between the two of you. If he listens to you, you have won your brother over. But if he will not listen, take one or two others along, so that 'every matter may be established by the testimony of two or three witnesses.' If he refuses to listen to them, tell it to the church; and if he refuses to listen even to the church, treat him as you would a pagan or a tax collector. I tell you the truth, whatever you bind on earth will be bound in heaven, and whatever you loose on earth will be loosed in heaven. Again, I tell you that if two of you on earth agree about anything you ask for, it will be done for you by My Father in heaven. For where two or three come together in My name, there am I with them." Then Peter came to Jesus and asked, "Lord, how many times shall I forgive my brother when he sins against me? Up to seven times?" Jesus answered, "I tell you, not seven times, but seventy-seven times." "Therefore, the kingdom of heaven is like a king who wanted to settle accounts with his servants. As he began the settlement, a man who owed him ten thousand talents was brought to him. Since he was not able to pay, the master ordered that he and his wife and his children and all that he had be sold to repay the debt. The servant fell on his knees before him. 'Be patient with*

me,' he begged, 'and I will pay back everything.' The servant's master took pity on him, cancelled the debt, and let him go. But when that servant went out, he found one of his fellow servants who owed him a hundred denarii. He grabbed him and began to choke him. 'Pay back what you owe me!' he demanded. His fellow servant fell to his knees and begged him, 'Be patient with me, and I will pay you back.' But he refused. Instead, he went off and had the man thrown into prison until he could pay the debt. When the other servants saw what had happened, they were greatly distressed and went and told their master everything that had happened. Then the master called the servant in. 'You wicked servant,' he said, 'I cancelled all that debt of yours because you begged me to. Shouldn't you have had mercy on your fellow servant just as I had on you?' In anger his master turned him over to the jailers to be tortured, until he should pay back all he owed. This is how My heavenly Father will treat each of you unless you forgive your brother from your heart."

The article argues that the central idea of this passage in the Book of Matthew, contained in verses 21-22, is best interpreted in light of the sections immediately preceding (verses 15-20) and immediately following (verses 23-35). These two sections give us implied qualifiers for verses 21-22 that disciples of Jesus would have understood, but that we often miss. This article concludes with the reminder that the extension of forgiveness is essentially related to the well-being of the believer in this life and the next.

What Is the Role of the Church?

Sadly, many churches nationwide as well as worldwide are ignorant of the impact of mental illness and the detrimental effects it can have on individuals, their families, and society as a whole. Some churches adopt an inflexible approach toward mentally illness and can be quite rigid in their repertoire toward someone sitting in their pews with some sort of mental disorder. Very sadly and most importantly, some churches fail to recognize that Jesus' ministry was also aimed at healing people with mental illness and demon possessions—as His ministry was and is based on devout love toward humankind. Some churches are well busy in building the Body of Christ by being spirit-filled, but they are producing a new generation of leaders who are shortsighted in their approach toward someone in their congregation who—as a result of psychosocial circumstances, errors in their thought life, or a traumatic event—is suffering from emotional or mental health problems. The issue of mental health is without a doubt a sorely neglected territory within some churches.

It seems that theology and medicine are at opposite poles about some health problems. It's easy for a church to accept someone with heart disease, cancer, diabetes, or a physically disability, but it is difficult to accept someone with mental health problems. One reason, I suppose, is a lack of understanding by church leaders about mental health problems—they feel as if they are not properly skilled to handle people with these issues. Some may think of them as time-wasters because they need to help themselves or that God cannot do anything for them and thus limit God's unlimited potential. There is lack of skilled training in pastoral counseling and a stigma attached to mental health problems.

I have attended many healing services in different churches and have seen many healings and live miracles of physically sick individuals, but I have yet to see mental health issues being given any due importance. The church, at times, has equated salvation with "being saved," while neglecting the dimension of being healed or making whole, which the root *salvus* denotes. The message conveyed by the healing stories in the New Testament is that the Kingdom of God would come as the healing power on earth. One basic function that is impaired in a mentally ill person is his or her ability to give and receive love.

As mentioned in the Preface, a teacher of psychiatry has observed that the two great commandments of Jesus provide a test of mental health. If a person is able to love God and neighbor, he is mentally healthy. When we see the basic purpose of the church and the nature of mental health in juxtaposition, their interrelationship becomes clear. *To say to a person who is crippled in his ability to love, "What you need is to love God and your neighbor," is like saying to a man clinging to a log in mid-ocean, "What you need is dry land." Nothing could be truer or less helpful.* In working for positive mental health or for the improved treatment of personality problems, the church is implementing its basic purpose by enhancing the ability of persons to love God and neighbor. I see local churches sometimes operating as a polite, middle-class, club- comfortable—but irrelevant to human agony.

For the sake of its spiritual integrity, the church must take an interest in the problems of mental illness. The inspiration and encouragement, fellowship, and sense of belonging to a family that come from involvement in the life of a church where people are "members one of another" (Rom. 12:5 KJV) is an important source of psychological nourishment. There needs to be creative partnership of inspiration, care, and commitment to people with mental health problems in the churches, and church leaders should create an atmosphere and a culture of reducing stigma associated with these issues—their interpersonal dynamics must be covered with love. Churches should provide person-centered ministries, and programs for potential church leaders should include person-centered training with regard to mental health and effective application of counseling skills.

COMMON MENTAL AND EMOTIONAL HEALTH PROBLEMS

The following are brief highlights of some common disorders and conditions that can affect our mental health.

Anxiety Disorders

Anxiety disorders are the most common and frequently occurring mental disorder and can transpire in an individual in a different ways. However, the core feature of these disorders remains anxiety symptoms and can affect our thinking, behavior, and physiological functions. Anxiety and worry symptoms are reactions to stress of day-to-day life. We all worry from time to time, and this is absolutely normal. However, when worries and anxieties dominate life, this is not normal. Excessive anxiety and worry significantly affects an individual on various domains in his or her psychosocial life. This can have an impact on relationships, careers, family life, and can torment a person's life to an extent of experiencing hell where there is deep anguish and pain.

Anxiety disorders include: panic disorders, generalized anxiety disorders, agoraphobia, specific phobia, obsessive-compulsive disorder, post traumatic stress disorder, and acute stress reactions. Anxiety and depressive symptoms often occur together. Symptoms of anxiety include: fearful anticipation of something bad or terrible going to happen, becoming more irritable, sensitivity to noise, poor concentration, and worrying thoughts. These symptoms can coexist with physical symptoms of dry mouth, excessive wind, difficulty inhaling, discomfort in chest, awareness of missed heartbeats, muscle tension, sleep disturbance, and appetite disturbance.

Generalized anxiety disorders can start in relation to some stressful event, and some will become chronic. People with anxiety disorders tend to catastrophize and worry unproductively about problems and they focus only on potentially threatening circumstances. Obsessive-compulsive disorders are feelings of subjective compulsion that must be resisted to carry out some action, to dwell on an idea, to recall an experience, or ruminate on an abstract topic. The obsessional urge or idea is recognized as alien to the personality but as coming from within the self. Obsessional thoughts are words, ideas, and beliefs, recognized by people as their own that intrude forcibly into the mind and are usually unpleasant. These thoughts can further be obscene or blasphemous or can be in the form of images, for example abnormal sexual practices. Many are preoccupied with details, rules, list, order, and schedules. Some are trying to be perfectionists, which interferes with task completion. Others might be unreasonable and insist that others submit to their way of doing things. People who suffer from these symptoms are usually secretive about their problems because of shame about their obsession and compulsion.

Ask yourself the following questions:

- ➤ Do you have thoughts, ideas, or mental images that come into your mind that you cannot seem to get rid of?

- ➤ Do these thoughts trouble you and make you feel anxious?

- ➤ Are there behaviors or activities you do repeatedly over which you have no control?

- ➤ Do you find that you tend to collect things excessively or have trouble throwing things out so that your home becomes cluttered?

- ➤ Do you find yourself touching, rubbing, or picking at parts of your body repeatedly?

- ➤ Are there any aspects of your appearance that you find yourself troubled by or preoccupied with?

If you answered yes to most or perhaps all of the questions, then you need to seek professional input.

Similarly, people who suffer from post traumatic stress have mind-sets that dwell on the trauma they experienced, which was of possibly life-threatening magnitude, and the person must respond with intense fear, helplessness, or horror. They have repeated flashbacks; and people suffering from this will usually avoid places, people, or events that might remind them of the event. People suffer other associated problems of survivor's guilt; they have disturbed interpersonal relationships, and display impulsive and self-destructive behavior.

Depressive Disorders

Depressive illness is common and causes severe disability in day-to-day functioning of an individual. Depression certainly is among the five most common disorders seen by physicians. Unrecognized and untreated depression has been acknowledged as a major public health problem. According to Medical Outcomes Study,[9] the disability caused by depression rivals that of coronary heart disease and is greater than the disability resulting from chronic lung disease or arthritis. Everyone will at some time in their lives be affected by depression—their own or someone else's, according to Australian government statistics. (Depression statistics in Australia are comparable to those of the USA and UK.)

The rate of increase of depression among children is an astounding 23 percent per annum, and 15 percent of the population of most developed countries suffer severe depression. Thirty percent of women are depressed. Men's figures were previously thought to be half that of women, but new estimates are higher. Fifty-four percent of people believe depression is a personal weakness. Forty-one percent of depressed women are too embarrassed to seek help. Fifteen percent of depressed people will commit suicide. There is a fourfold increase in deaths in individuals with this disorder who are over age 55. Individuals with this disorder have more pain and physical illness and decreased physical, social, and role functioning. Depression will be the second largest killer after heart disease by 2020—and studies show depression is a contributory factor to fatal coronary disease. Overall, depression occurs in 1 in 10 adults. It is argued that men tend to express their symptoms differently, for example, through the use of alcohol and drugs, and are unwilling to admit to the symptoms of depression.[10]

Causes of Depression

Depression can be due to biological mechanisms, genetic predisposition, biochemical disturbances, some medications, and psychological errors in processing information perceived through the external environment. Acute events that can cause depressive symptoms include marital breakdown, job loss, physical illness, and financial difficulties. Past experiences can affect the way we feel about ourselves in the present, and if that feeling is negative it can have a long-term effect. People with certain personality traits are more likely to become depressed. These include negative thinking, pessimism, excess worry, low self-esteem, a hypersensitivity to perceived rejection, overdependence on others, a sense of superiority or alienation from others, and ineffective responses to stress. Difficult life events, loss, change, or persistent stress can cause levels of neurotransmitters to become unbalanced, leading to depression. While it has long been believed that depression caused people to misuse alcohol and drugs in an attempt to make themselves feel better (self-medication), it is now thought that the reverse can also be the case; substance abuse can actually cause depression.

Symptoms of Depression

Clinical depression is not something you feel for a day or two before feeling better. In true depression, the symptoms last weeks, months, or sometimes years if you don't seek treatment. If you are depressed, you are often unable to perform daily activities. You may not care enough to get out of bed or get dressed, much less work, do errands, or socialize. If you have the following symptoms and they are persistent and if the feelings do not go away, then most likely you are the victim of clinical depression:

➤ Feeling low in mood nearly every day.

➤ Loss of interest in doing things you enjoyed before.

➤ Sleep disturbance.

- Appetite change.

- Weight loss or gain.

- Fatigue.

- Loss of energy.

- Poor concentration.

- Recurrent morbid thoughts of suicide.

- Poor outlook on life.

- Pessimistic about everything.

- Guilt feelings, self-blame, feeling tearful.

Children with depression may exhibit these same symptoms, which can lead to poor school performance, persistent boredom, frequent complaints of physical problems; teenagers may show depression by taking more risks and/or showing less concern for their own safety.

If you suspect that you are not feeling well in your mood or if someone makes a comment regarding your mood, it is important that you seek help. Do not wait for it to get worse or out of control. I have seen many people suffer in silence. If you are one of them, make sure you do something about it. You may perhaps find it useful to have a chat with a friend or someone you can confide in, and also seek professional help.

Bipolar Disorders

Bipolar disorder is basically the other end of the pendulum of depression. In this condition the primary symptoms are of being high or elated in mood. Although being high is not bad in itself. When I am in the presence of God, I can be anointed with the Holy Spirit and experience a high in my spirit. However, if being high causes disruptions in your social, occupational, or family life, this is considered abnormal. There is a cyclical variation in mood, cognition, and behavior for people with bipolar disorders. People with manic-depression often exhibit an elated or irritable mood, which is associated with an inflated self-esteem, difficulty sleeping, full of energy, increased activity, flight of ideas, engaging in risk-taking behavior, whether being sexual impulsivity or overspending, and this usually causes painful consequences.

You may be surprised that some stressors are statistically more likely to be associated with the onset of manic episodes. Interpersonal and work difficulties are common precipitants associated with mood destabilization. Sleep deprivation may be a final common pathway that leads to mania in a variety of situations. Since a manic episode can quickly escalate and destroy a patient's career or reputation, a therapist must be prepared to hospitalize out-of-control manic patients before they "lose everything." Likewise, severely depressed, suicidal bipolar patients often require hospitalization to save their lives.

Psychotic Disorders

Psychotic disorders include severe mental disorders characterized by extreme impairment of a person's ability to think clearly, respond emotionally, communicate effectively, understand reality, and behave appropriately.

These are the disorders that can manifest in an individual as schizophrenic illness, paranoid disorder, delusional disorders, etc. These disorders commonly cause abnormal thinking and perception. People lose touch with reality. In extreme cases where their thought life is going completely volatile and out of control, they will be more at risk of developing a network of belief systems in their mind that even to any reasonable rationalization, will be held in their mind as if it is really real. I have read about many men and women developing pathological jealousy to a degree that they start to doubt the integrity of their partner and they end up in divorce or separation. In worst-case scenarios, this can lead to homicide or suicide.

Two of the main symptoms psychotic disorders are delusions and hallucinations. *Delusions* are false belief systems that cannot be shifted by any reasonable explanation. For example, in grandiose delusions, a person's belief about his/her own importance or station in life is grossly out of proportion to what is really true. For instance, a person might believe that he or she is Jesus Christ. *Hallucinations* are false perceptions such as hearing, seeing, or feeling something that is not there. Some people will suffer from brief reactive psychosis, which is a sudden, short-term display of psychotic behavior, such as hallucinations that occur with a stressful event.

Some people's psychotic episodes are solely associated as direct results of illicit drug use or excessive alcohol intake. In our modern-day society, a culture of drugs and alcohol is common, and some parents even condone such behavior in their teenage children, thinking that it is OK for them to use illegal drugs or drink alcohol. These young kids' mind-sets are so influenced by their peers, and in some cases by their parents, that to safeguard their egos, they engage in harmful activities that can provoke a chain of psychotic reactions.

Psychotic disorders are actually quite common worldwide. About 1 percent of the population is thought to have some form of psychotic disorder.[11] Possible symptoms of psychotic illnesses include:

- ➤ Disorganized or incoherent speech.

- ➤ Confused thinking.

- ➤ Strange, possibly dangerous behavior.

- ➤ Slowed or unusual movements.

- ➤ Loss of interest in personal hygiene.

- ➤ Loss of interest in activities.

- ➤ Problems at school or work and with relationships.

- ➤ Cold, detached manner with the inability to express emotion.

- ➤ Mood swings or other mood symptoms, such as depression or mania.

As you know by now, our mind-sets and emotions have great influence over our mental health. In the next chapter, personality disorders are discussed as well as demon possession and suicide. Shedding light on these subjects that people would rather not think about is vital so you can be aware of symptoms that may be serious and to identify warning signs in yourself or others.

ENDNOTES

1. Office of National Statistics-UK; http://www.statistics. gov.uk/cci/nugget.asp?id=1092; accessed May 13, 2010.

2. Focus on Mental Health-UK; www.statistics.gov.uk/downloads/theme.../09_MentalHealth.pdf.

3. "Mental Health Costs Soar," http://www.medicalnewstoday.com/articles/160216.php; accessed April 29, 2010.

4. Laura Gibson, "Look after your mental health on World Mental Health Day," October 2005; http://www.ebility. com/articles/world-mental-health-day.php; accessed May 13, 2010.

5. Jane M. Voon Bergen, "Survey find mental-health troubles rise in jobless," October 7, 2009; http://www.philly.com/ philly/jobs/20091007_Survey_finds_mental-health_troubles_rise_in_jobless.html; accessed May 13, 2010.

6. http://www.answers.com/topic/erik-erikson; accessed May 13, 2010.

7. Kendra Cherry, "Erikson's Theory of Psychosocial Development," http://psychology.about.com/od/theoriesofpersonality/a/psychosocial.htm; accessed May 13, 2010.

8. www.thejpc.net/category/psychology-and-biblical-scholarship; Journal of psychology & Christianity.

9. A.R. Tarlov, et. al., "The Medical Outcomes Study. An application of methods for monitoring the results of medical care," (JAMA 1989 Aug 18;262(7):925-30); http://www. ncbi.nlm.nih.gov/pubmed/2754793; accessed May 13, 2010.

10. "Statistics 1: How common is mental disorder?"; http:// www.mind.org.uk/help/research_and_policy/statistics_1_h ow_common_is_mental_distress; accessed May 13, 2010.

11. http://www.ncbi.nlm.nih.gov/bookshelf/br.fcgi?book =hssamhsatip&part=A30406.

Chapter 5

Personality Disorders and Demon Possession

Our personalities are made up of the way we think, feel, and behave. By our late teens or early 20s, we have developed our own personalities. We function better within our core belief system and this transpires into our personalities and relationships. Our personalities help us get along reasonably well with other people.

However, unhelpful ways of thinking, feeling, and behaving will certainly cause problems with your personality. Personality disorders are long-term patterns of thoughts and behaviors that cause serious problems with relationships and work. People with personality disorders have difficulty dealing with everyday stresses and problems. They often have stormy relationships with other people. The exact cause of personality disorders is unknown. However, genes and childhood experiences may play a role.

General signs and symptoms that may indicate a personality disorder include:

> ➤ Frequent mood swings.

> ➤ Stormy relationships.

> ➤ Social isolation.

> ➤ Angry outbursts.

> ➤ Suspicion and mistrust of others.

- ➤ Difficulty making friends.

- ➤ A need for instant gratification.

- ➤ Poor impulse control.

- ➤ Alcohol or substance abuse.

Personality Disorder Types

For the benefit of easy understanding, I have classified personality disorders according to three clusters:

A. Odd/eccentric: includes people with paranoid, schizoid types.

B. Dramatic/erratic: includes borderline, antisocial, histrionic, and narcissistic.

C. Anxious/fearful: includes avoidant, dependent, and obsessive-compulsive types.

Cluster A group have general distrust of others, misinterpretation of others' actions, odd beliefs, and a tendency toward social isolation. These types of personalities are hostile and cause conflicts. They are emotionally detached from others, exhibit lack of interest in social interaction, have flat emotions, and live believing that they can influence people and events with their thoughts.

Cluster B group exhibit unstable, unpredictable, unlikable, and impulsive symptoms. They take risks, display volatile moods, suicidal behavior, recurring legal difficulties, and persistent lying or stealing. On the other hand, they want to be the center of attention, seek others' approval, expect constant praise and admiration, fail to recognize other people's emotions, excessive concern with physical appearance, and fantasize about power, success, and happiness. These people have difficulty establishing and maintaining interpersonal relationships.

Cluster C group are often anxious, timid, perfectionists, and conflict-avoidant; presentation frequently triggered by depression or somatic complaints. They are hypersensitive to criticism or rejection, feel inadequate, have excessive dependence on others, and feel an urgent need to start a new relationship if one has ended. People with obsessive-compulsive personality are preoccupied with perfectionism and rules, exhibit a desire to be in control of situations, and are unable to discard broken or worthless objects.

Remember, personality is the combination of thoughts, emotions, and behaviors that make you unique. It's the way you view, understand, and relate to the outside world, as well as how you see yourself. Personality disorders are common worldwide, affecting about 10 to 13 percent of people at some point during their lives.[1]

Complications of ongoing personality disorders include:

- ➤ Depression and anxiety symptoms or disorders.

- ➤ Suicidal tendencies and self-harming behavior.

- ➤ Eating disorders.

- ➤ Impulsivity.

- ➤ Disinhibition on behavior.

- ➤ Reckless behavior.

- ➤ Risky sexual behavior.

- ➤ Child abuse.

- ➤ Illicit drug use and alcohol abuse/dependence.

- ➤ Aggression or violence.

- ➤ Incarceration.

- ➤ Relationship difficulties.

- ➤ Social isolation.

- ➤ School and work problems.

- ➤ Strained relationships with health care providers.

POST TRAUMATIC STRESS DISORDER

Post traumatic stress disorder (PTSD) happens after intense, prolonged, and sometimes delayed reaction to an intensely stressful event.

People suffering from PTSD symptoms have hyper arousal, re-experiences of aspects of stressful events, and avoidance of reminders. Examples of extreme stressors are natural disasters, manmade calamities such as serious accidents or terrorist activities, and rape or serious physical assault. Common symptoms underlying PTSD are persistent anxiety, irritability, difficulty sleeping, poor concentration, flashbacks of incident, and diminished interest in activities. Due to the impact of the catastrophic event, many people develop maladaptive coping responses, which include persistent aggressive behavior, excessive use of alcohol or drugs, and deliberate self-harm and suicide. Very commonly, people with PTSD are overwhelmed by emotionally charged information so that the memories persist in an unprocessed form and can intrude into conscious awareness.

Victims of rape or physical assault experience acute reactions to stress, PTSD symptoms, anxiety and depressive disorders, and psychosexual dysfunction. As well as symptoms of PTSD, people who go through severe trauma also feel humiliated, ashamed, and vulnerable to further attack. They lose confidence, self-esteem, and commonly go through a cycle of self-blame and pessimism about their future.

Eating Disorders

Eating disorders develop due to abnormalities in patterns of eating that are determined primarily by the attitude a person has regarding his or her weight and shape. Again, a vital ingredient here is a distorted thinking pattern. Many eating disorders go clinically unrecognized, and it is estimated that only about half of the cases of anorexia nervosa in the population are detected in primary care. For bulimia nervosa, the figure is substantially less and many individuals with bulimia are untreated. When anorexia sets in, people can have mood swings, rigid thinking, and be controlling and manipulative. Major defense mechanisms include denial of their illness and intellectualization. Their thinking becomes black-and-white or good-versus-bad without the capacity to integrate the two. They can become mistrustful of others, strive for perfection, have obsessive-compulsive personalities, and become socially isolated. However, bulimics can be superficially sociable and perceived by others as strong and giving. Unfortunately, they have problems with low self-esteem and conflicts with intimacy, feel misunderstood, and have difficulty managing anger.

IMPULSE CONTROL DISORDERS

Impulse control disorders are a loosely grouped set of conditions that have in common a central feature behavior that is acted out in an uncontrolled and impulsive manner that often has self-destructive consequences. Many psychiatric disorders are associated with impulsive aggression, but some individuals demonstrate violent outbursts of rage, which are variously referred to as rage attacks, anger attacks, episodic dyscontrol, or intermittent explosive disorder. Intermittent explosive disorder was first formally conceptualized as a psychiatric disorder. These disorders also include kleptomania (stealing), pathological gambling, pyromania (fire starting), trichotillomania (pulling one's hair out), and dermatillomania (skin picking). Each impulse control disorder has varying symptoms. Many include features of "tension and release," where increasing levels of anxiety are experienced prior to the act, and feelings of pleasure, gratification or relief are experienced after the act.

Each individual impulse control disorder has different symptoms. However, there are some symptoms common to all impulse control disorders, not elsewhere classified, regardless of the focus of the impulsive behavior. These include:

- Strong urges to engage in a behavior that may be damaging to oneself or to others.

- Inability to resist engaging in the behavior. In some cases, feelings of tension, anxiety, and irritability occur in an attempt to avoid these impulses.

- Preoccupation with the behavior.

- Experiencing distress or impairment (emotional, interpersonal, financial), arrest, and physical injury as result of the behavior.

We all go through impulses in which our feelings are connected to an action. In other words we have an urge to act. When we are able to control our impulses and hinder their conversion into actions, we may have adequate defenses. However, if our defenses are weak, we may start to leak our feelings through our actions.

Intermittent Explosive Disorder

Intermittent explosive disorder (IED) is recurrent and distinct episodes of aggressive behavior that cause harm to others or the destruction of property. These episodes are not preceded by feelings of building tension. Instead, they are sudden outbursts, which are grossly out of proportion to their trigger. The aggressive impulses and acts may be accompanied by increased energy, racing thoughts, and feelings of uncontrollable rage. Chronic aggression is often present in patients with Cluster B personality disorders (borderline, antisocial, narcissistic, histrionic) as described previously. In IED, there are several episodes of aggression that result in serious destruction or assault and are not better accounted for by other psychiatric disorders. Basically, people cannot keep their rage under control. They show a calm attitude to the outside world, but inside they are reaching a melting point where they need to explode and release the gases. Perhaps they are projecting these unhealthy emotions or impulses onto their partner and children—there can be a serious issue of domestic violence behind their closed doors.

Anything that causes disruption in your ego will cause you to put on armor of defense and brew up argument that can take a spiral downward course of destruction. I have seen many people with mental health problems in my clinic who are suffering from a severe degree of stress and mental health breakdown. One thing noticeable from their clinical history is that they have difficulty with interpersonal relationships. Many of these individuals have generalized anger management problems, and they tend to control their anger outside the four walls of their home. Individuals who have no control over their emotions in a relationship will attach emotional ultimatums whenever they have conflict. Within a relationship, each person has expectations from another person, and if these expectations are not up to required standards, then they tend to start a roller coaster cycle of interpersonal emotional battle.

If you find yourself acting in ways that seem out of control and frightening, you may need help finding better ways to deal with this emotion.

Cognitive Restructuring

Simply put, cognitive restructuring means changing the way you think. Angry people tend to curse, swear, or speak in highly colorful terms that reflect their inner thoughts. When you're angry, your thinking can become very exaggerated and overly dramatic. Try replacing these thoughts with more rational ones. For instance, instead of telling yourself, "Oh, it's awful, it's terrible, everything's ruined," tell yourself, "This is frustrating, and it's understandable that I'm upset about it, but it's not the end of the world and getting angry is not going to fix it anyhow." You may also need to develop better communication skills along with assertiveness. Try to avoid judging others and deal with your pride. You may also need to learn to think carefully before you say the first thing that comes to your mind. Words spoken in anger can cause damage to the listener. Therefore, you need to pause, think, and rationalize before speaking.

Developing strategies to find a solution to the problem that is upsetting you in first place is also very helpful. Stop putting up a defensive front, and look at the problem to see if you are the one who is actually the cause and the consequence. One of the most important aspects of controlling your anger against someone who has hurt you is to release that person in forgiveness and do not hold a grudge. If you plant a seed of bitterness and revenge, in due course it will release its poison and can affect many lives. This poison can also cost someone his or her life. I know that it is very difficult to forgive someone who has done a lot of damage to your emotional and mental well-being. But if you are nurturing bitterness, it will consume your life and mind, and you will be at risk of adopting a victim's mentality. Use humor to release tensions. Lightening up can help diffuse tension. Don't use sarcasm, though—it can hurt feelings and make things worse.

Forgiveness has numerous health benefits including:

> ➤ Reduces stress and depressive symptoms.

> ➤ Lowers your blood pressure.

> ➤ Reduces anxiety-related symptoms.

> ➤ Lowers use of alcohol and drugs.

> ➤ Reduces chronic pain.

> ➤ Increases social connections.

> ➤ Improves psychological well-being.

❯ Increases sense of peace and spiritual well-being.

❯ Contributes to better anger management.

When you hold on to unforgiveness, bitterness, revenge, hatred, jealousy, and anger, it overspills into your life, relationships, and affects you emotionally. Unforgiveness can make you: dwell on the event surrounding the offense, avoid family and friends, use illicit drugs or alcohol to cope with pain, have automatic thoughts of negativity about any given situation, have difficulty sleeping, exhibit depression and anxiety symptoms, lose relationships, and have feelings that you are always misunderstood. You need to forgive all those who have wronged you in order to release yourself from the dominion of anger, bitterness, unforgiveness, and other such things.

Forgiveness may be sincerely spoken words such as, "I forgive you" or tender actions that fit the relationship. But more than this, forgiveness brings peace that helps you go on with life. The offense is no longer front and center in your thoughts or feelings. Your hostility, resentment, and misery have made way for compassion, kindness, and peace. Remember that by forgiving others you have set yourself free from being a victim and it takes away the power that the other person continually wielded upon you. Accept the fact that you—like everyone else—aren't perfect. Accept yourself despite your faults. Admit your mistakes. Commit to treating others with compassion, empathy, and respect. And again, talking with a spiritual leader, mental health provider, or trusted friend or relative may be helpful.

Demon Possession and Mental Health

The Bible clearly recognizes that not all illnesses are attributable to demons. Matthew 4:23 says Jesus healed all diseases and delivered those possessed of demons.

In the *Journal of Religion & Health* in 2005, the author highlights that evidence of evil spirits is voluminous and comes from many cultures, both ancient and modern.[2] Cases from China, India, and the United States are examined and evaluated. The actual experience of spirit victims, the universality of spirit oppression, the superhuman phenomena associated with possession, and the comparative success of deliverance and exorcism versus psychiatry are considered. Potential arguments are presented against the spirit hypothesis center on the antecedent improbability of spirits, multiple personality disorder, and the effectiveness of medication. Mental illness is strictly a matter of an aberrant brain, carefully examine the literature of possession, experiment to determine why exorcists and deliverance ministers often succeed where psychiatry fails, and develop a more complete inventory of techniques for healing the complete person.

However, at the same time you need to bear in mind that not all mental illnesses are a result of demonic possession or influence. It is very prevalent in today's church world that if someone is suffering from mental illness, they are viewed as being demon possessed. In theological and Bible schools worldwide, not much curriculum covers the psychological aspects of mental illnesses and instead they tend to primarily focus on demonic influence rather than looking at the medical and psychosocial aspects of mental illness. There are various disorders that may mimic demonic possession including schizophrenia, dissociative identity disorder, and Tourette syndrome.

Psychiatry has begun to acknowledge possession disorder in a small way. In the International Classification of Disease (ICD-10), there is now a classification for trance and possession disorder. In general, though, many psychiatrists regard demon possession as a relic of pre-scientific superstition. Demon possession and mental illness, then, are not simply alternative diagnoses. Furthermore, demon possession is essentially a spiritual problem, but mental illness is a multi-factorial affair, in which spiritual, social, psychological, and physical factors may all play a role in the cause or origin. It is important to understand the symptoms caused by demon possession or oppression and how these symptoms can relate to mental illness. A person presenting with repeated self-harming behavior or may present with acute psychotic episode should not be construed as caused by demons; however, in differential diagnosis we should not completely rule these out either.

Dissociative identity disorder, or multiple personality disorder, are terms very widely used in psychiatry. This is when there is a presence of two or more distinct identities, or personality states, that take control of a person.

The following are the *symptoms* that can be due to demonic oppression:

- Lack of self-control.
- Abnormal fear and anxieties.
- Conflict with authority figures.
- Aimlessness.
- Outburst of violence.
- Outburst of hatred.
- Irrationality.

These are the *causes* of the demonic oppression:

- Sexual immorality.
- Pornographic addiction that recurs continuously.
- Hedonism.
- Participation in false religion, cults, or black or white magic.
- Preoccupation with occult and other rituals.
- Anger against God and others.
- Persistent jealousy.
- Bad temper.
- Thrill seeking in alcohol, drugs, and night clubs.

Symptoms of demonic possession include:

- Strange physical ailments or disfigurement.
- Verbal outburst, mostly obscene.
- Violent and vulgar behavior.
- Body spasms and contortions.
- Ability to speak languages never learned before.

- ➤ Self-harming.

- ➤ Superhuman abilities.

- ➤ Irreverent, vile, lewd comments about members of the Godhead; comments attributing gross sexual immorality to Jesus.

- ➤ Severe, persistent depression, despondency, and/or temptations to commit suicide.

- ➤ Cessation of normal bodily functions for a period of time.

Possession trance is characterized by a transient alteration in identity whereby one's normal identity is temporarily replaced (possessed) by a spirit, ghost, deity, or other person. The experience of being "possessed" by another entity, such as a person, god, demon, animal, or inanimate object, holds different meanings in different cultures; and therefore, the diagnosis for this disorder may be culturally bound. While possession is a common experience in many cultures, in Western industrialized cultures, such experiences are not the norm.

Therefore, it is clear that there is a close link between certain manifestations of psychiatrically unexplained symptoms that can only be better accounted for by different mechanisms. However, at the same time, a genuine mental disorder or emotional problem should not be labeled as demon possession. Mental health professionals and church leaders need to recognize these thorny issues and must set aside their differences. I believe they should integrate mental health and spiritual dimensions in any individual suspected to be under demonic influence.

SUICIDE

Suicide is the act of intentionally killing oneself. Suicide has many determinants, but it is always an attempt to solve a problem. The likelihood of a person dying by suicide depends on several factors such as, mental illness, social problems-family problems, separation, divorce, and ease of access to the means of suicide. Asking patients to describe what they think would happen if they killed themselves may elicit wishes for revenge, punishment, power, control, escape, rebirth, reunion with the dead, or a new life. Ultimately, a person's mind controls whether or not he or she commits suicide. Suicide is among the ten leading causes of death in most countries. In Great Britain, it is the third most important contributor to life-year lost after coronary heart disease and cancer.

Ninety to 95 percent of suicide victims suffer from a psychiatric illness at the time they die. People who suffer from major depression, hopelessness, schizophrenia, borderline personality disorder, alcohol dependence, and bipolar disorder are particularly at an increased risk of dying by suicide. In England and Wales, in 2001, hanging was the most commonly used method for suicide by men, followed by drug overdose and self-poisoning by car exhaust fumes. In the USA, gunshot and other violent methods are more commonly used to commit suicide.[3]

Most completed suicides have been planned beforehand and most of the time the person leaves a note behind for others to find. In one study done in the UK, two-thirds of people who committed suicide had consulted their general practitioner for some reason in the previous month and a quarter of them were seeing a psychiatrist.[4]

Suicide Causes

Medical and psychiatric problems as mentioned are the common causes behind the state of mind before executing suicide.

Social factors such as unemployment, poverty, divorce, and social fragmentation have higher rates of suicide. Sometimes fictional television programs and films depicting suicide can be linked to higher suicide risk. People at high risk of suicide display signs of hopelessness, impulsivity, dichotomous thinking, cognitive constriction, and problem-solving deficits.

There is a battle raging daily in our minds, and to keep the victory on our side, we must learn how to control the thoughts volleying back and forth. Strategies that will help you win the battle for your mind are presented in the following chapter. The strategies described demonstrate how you can live a victorious life every day.

ENDNOTES

1. Mayo clinic staff, "Personality Disorders: Risk Factors," http://www.mayoclinic.com/health/personality-disorders/DS00562/DSECTION=risk-factors; accessed May 13, 2010.

2. Betty Stafford, "The Growing Evidence for Demonic Possession: What Should Psychiatry's Response Be?;" *Journal of Religion & Health*, Vol. 44, (April 1, 2005), 13-30 (18).

3. Markus Grobe, et. al., "Medico legal evaluation of suicidal deaths," February 2010; http://www.springerlink.com/content/tw81334l50575100/; accessed May 13, 2010.

4. Philip Meats and Bohdan Solomka, "A Perspective of Suicide in the 90s," *The Psychiatrist* (1995), 19: 666-669. doi: 10.1192/pb.19.11.666.

Chapter 6

Strategies to Win the Mind Battle

To have victory in any battle, a soldier must strategize along with his team to defend his base and attack the enemy. This is of vital importance in order to win the battle. As we read in previous chapters, our minds can process thoughts and feelings and convert them into behavioral action. We also know that the causes of suffering, our thought life, and most importantly a victim's mentality and psychological impact can affect our lives dramatically.

You don't have to live in same old rut; you can change your thought life to claim victory over any problems you may be facing today. Today is your day to say no to your old self and say yes to positive changes in your life. You are now going to condemn your negative thoughts forever and start a life of confidence, assertiveness, and high self-esteem. You will not break into pieces when faced with any problem; instead, you will deal with the problem head-on and move forward with your life.

"Winners in life think constantly in terms of 'I can, I will, and I am.' Losers, on the other hand, concentrate their waking thoughts on what they should have or would have done, or what they can't do."[1] I am challenging you right now to never be afraid to do something new. Denis Waitley also says, "There are two primary choices in life; to accept conditions as they exist, or accept the responsibility for changing them."[2] Mind is all that counts. You can be whatever you make up your mind to be. More powerful than the will to win is the courage to begin.

I firmly believe that the only real failure in life is the failure to try. Life is a book with many chapters. Some tell of tragedy, others of triumph. Some chapters are dull and ordinary, others intense and exciting. The key to being a success in life is to never stop on a difficult page, to never quit during a tough chapter. Champions have the courage to keep turning the pages because they know a better chapter lies ahead—and with God, nothing is impossible. Martin Luther King Jr. said, "The ultimate measure of a person is not where they stand in moments of comfort and convenience, but where the stand in times of challenge and controversy."[3]

I want you to begin with a mind-set of achieving success before I give you some practical strategies to conquer negative thoughts that are producing intense emotion and causing you to fail in every area of your life. Begin with saying this positive reaffirmation:

"I am going to change my mind-set and I will change my victim's mentality through Christ Jesus who already defeated sin and carnality. From this day forward I am going to lead a life of victory in my mind and control my thoughts for the best results in my life, relationships, career, my children's lives, and in my inner self. I claim peace and victory and success."

Now you can sow seeds of success. Success lies not in the result but in all the efforts. Being best is not at all-important; doing your best is all that matters. The very first ingredient you need to overcome any difficulties or obstacles is *determination*. Nobody trips over mountains. It is the small pebble that causes you to stumble. Step over all the pebbles in your path, and you will find you have crossed the mountain.

People are always blaming their circumstances for what they are. I don't believe in circumstances. The people who get on in this world are the people who get up and look for the circumstances they want; and, if they can't find them, make them. Look at the athletes who compete in the Olympic games. They put in lot of effort, hard work, endurance, stamina, and they remain focused on their objective. They have already developed a mind-set of winning the competition before they are even chosen to compete. They are determined to go into the competition with courage, and they persevere to come out victorious. Albert Einstein said, "There are only two ways to live your life. One is though nothing is a miracle. The other is though everything is a miracle."[4] Never bend your head. Always hold it high. Look the world straight in the face. You have got to say to yourself, "I am not going to be a slave to my negative emotions. I am going to master my negative emotions and drag them out of my mind so that I can have a positive and more disciplined lifestyle!"

What does it mean to succeed? Most people see success as being rich and famous or powerful and influential. Others see it as being at the top of their profession and standing out from the rest. *The wise see success in a more personal way; they see it as achieving the goals they have set for themselves, and then feeling pride and satisfaction in their accomplishments.* True success is felt in the heart, not measured by money and power. So be true to yourself and achieve the goals you set.

BEGIN YOUR JOURNEY BY DISCOVERING YOURSELF

Now is the time to self-evaluate yourself and your personality—to get to the bottom of yourself and dig out any unhealthy attitude and personality. Start now to strategize how you are going to eliminate unhealthy and unhelpful qualities from your life. You are in the middle of a battlefield with yourself and facing your worst enemy—YOU. Your worst enemy is bombarding you with thoughts like, "There is no point in doing this—I'll never succeed," "I'll never get out of this mess. I'm in too deep." When you are attacked by these types of thoughts, you become paralyzed. My thought life was like this before I finally decided to face up to my worst enemy—and that was ME. Try to define yourself and see yourself for real. What do you see in the mirror? A defeated man or a woman or a determined and self-disciplined person!

In order to improve and bring positive changes, you must first ascertain where you are and then where you want to be. If you aren't sure where you are, it is impossible to start making movements toward where you want to be. Therefore, it is of utmost importance for you to identify and discover your whole being. To begin this journey you need to be honest with yourself.

Be Honest With Yourself. Discovering yourself inevitably creates the paradoxical situation where you accept who you are without removing the desire to improve. You sometimes know exactly what you need to do to change the situation or problem that is troubling you, however, you are not willing to be flexible. Perhaps your pride is in your way or you are just very lazy about changing your lifestyle that hurts and is deeply painful. Speak with authority to your negative self and say, "I am no longer your slave!" Do not leave any room for negotiation with your negative self because your negative self never wants you to slip away. Your negative self hinders your path and can have a strong influence on your mind if you don't make it a point to keep it under control. You need to attack your negative subconscious and listen to your higher brain commands. The more you delete listening to your subconscious, the more likely you are to gain control over yourself and your thought life.

Write Your Personality. Write down anything that you associate with your identity. Look at the following list and see if you fit into one or more of any qualities. This means accomplishments, failures, strengths, weaknesses, personality traits, interests, hopes, past, future, etc. Keep writing until you can't think of anything more. Stick with the exercise until it is finished. This may take as long as twenty minutes or more if you are a slow writer, but it will give you immense clarity and satisfaction afterward. You will be very surprised at what you will uncover about yourself.

At this point, do not shy away from it. Whatever you have written is staring right back at you, and you are staring right into the eyes of your own downfall. You might feel uncomfortable writing down negative aspects about yourself. You may have pushed some of these traits away or avoided them. But part of discovering yourself is also finding the parts that you dislike, are afraid of, or even hate. Yes, you need to stare at them, and you need to start telling yourself, "This is junk in my life that needs to be shredded and burnt away." This is the best way to identify yourself as good or bad or ugly. Accept the truth that these are components of your identity. The next step is complete acceptance of this list. If you don't feel the list is complete, go back and add more to it, but ultimately you must look at your immense list of qualities and accept that this is who you are right now, in this very moment. You need to identify the core life traps that are holding you back from fulfilling your true nature.

Personality qualities:

Adaptability: Making changes when necessary.

Calmness: Being serene.

Carefulness: Giving watchful attention to people and/or things; making sure that you do things properly.

Compassion: Having sympathy and feelings for people with problems.

Compatibility: Being in harmony with others, and having the ability to work well with others.

Competitiveness: Striving to win.

Courage: Meeting danger or difficulties in spite of fear.

Courtesy: Being thoughtful of others.

Decisiveness: Making decisions promptly and definitely.

Dedication: Being seriously devoted to causes and/or goals.

Drive: Having the energy to get things done.

Enthusiasm: Having a strong affinity toward people and/or things; to show eagerness and a willingness to work with others or things.

Honesty: Having integrity and keeping your promise.

Industriousness: Being consistently active; getting your work done.

Influence: Motivating or encouraging others.

Initiative: Starting thoughts and/or actions.

Loyalty: Showing allegiance to people and/or things; showing devotion to your company, people, or things.

Open-mindedness: Being receptive and interested in the opinions and ideas of others.

Patience: Being able to wait; taking your time to do things.

Perfectionism: Trying to achieve the highest possible degree of excellence.

Perseverance: Being persistent in pursuit of tasks.

Responsibility: Being accountable for duties; and actually following through with your duties.

Self-control: Controlling your own actions and feelings.

Self-reliance: Having trust in yourself; doing things yourself and feeling confident about them.

Stability: Being constant in responses

Accept Reality. Your real power begins on the inside, with self-awareness and self-acceptance. Accept your incompleteness to become more complete; if you cannot change things, change your attitude; never lament what you cannot have; truly accept that you have enough of everything. Your real power is in staying creative and ready to adapt. Be a disciple of life—be soft and flexible, not a disciple of death—stiff and inflexible; see external change as an opportunity for self-improvement; make use of whatever happens. By questioning your assumptions, beliefs, and thoughts you will grow and succeed at a much faster rate. Our automatic thoughts and "conclusions" can hold us back if we are not conscious about examining them.

Bring Discipline Into Your Life. When you have discovered the layers of personality causing difficulties in your life, you need to exercise self-discipline to clean up the junk and clutter in your life, mind, and heart. Strive to achieve as many positive qualities and personalities as listed. *Self-discipline* involves acting according to what you *think* instead of how you *feel* in the moment. Often self-discipline involves sacrificing the pleasure and thrill of the moment for what matters most in life. Self-discipline depends upon conscious awareness as to both what you are doing and what you are not doing. Think about it. If you aren't aware, your behavior is undisciplined; how will you know to act otherwise? It is not enough to simply write out your goals and values. You must make an internal commitment to them. You also need to display good courage to be successful in achieving disciplined behavior and thought life. Moods, appetites, and passions can be powerful forces to go against. Therefore self-discipline is highly dependent on courage. Don't pretend something is easy for you to do when it is in fact very difficult and/or painful. Instead, find the courage to face the pain and difficulty. As you begin to accumulate small victories, your self-confidence will grow and the courage that underpins self-discipline will come more naturally.

Maintain Your Integrity. When you have become aware of your weaknesses and failures and when you have already faced up to your worst enemy, now is the time to display integrity in your thoughts and say to yourself, "I am going to be successful in creating a new me." There are many situations when doing something conflicts with your inner feelings or thoughts. Get into the habit of analyzing such situations. Quite often we conflict with our principles for the sake of looking good or making some progress. That's why it is very important to always make sure you know if such a sacrifice is really necessary. If it's something not important, you should never conflict with yourself, because in many situations you're acting a certain way simply because of the situation you're in. But when situations change, as they always do, you will be left on your own with your thoughts and conflicts.

Take Responsibility. *Not* taking responsibility may be less demanding, less painful, and mean less time spent in the unknown. It's more comfortable. You can just take it easy and blame problems in your life on someone else. But there is always a price to pay. When you don't take responsibility for your life, you give away your personal power. When you blame others, you give up your power to change. I find that many people suffer from a self-esteem problem and the big reason is that they don't want to take responsibility for their lives and actions. Instead, they blame someone else for everything wrong in their lives and hence they empower a victim's mentality to brew. Hurts will not stop until they wise up and take responsibility for their lives. You also need to stop relying on external validation like praise from other people to feel good about yourself. Believe in yourself that you are a human being created beautifully and wonderfully, and from this day forward you will delete the rubbish once and for all.

When you take responsibility, you will discover the Beautiful You who was hidden underneath your rigid, negative, and stinking personality. Write down the areas of your life you will start to take responsibility, and make sure you take one step at a time to be successful in your role. Take responsibility for your life and your environment, including your children, spouse, siblings, parents, and your work colleagues. Start listening to the authentic voice inside of you—your personality. When you start to play to your strengths, you can achieve success, peace, and joy.

At the same time, it is also important to know your limitations and how people are going to react to what you say or do. This is also very essential to discovering your identity.

List Your Priorities. Making a list of your priorities makes you think about what and who comes first, second, third, etc., in your life. I have seen marital breakdowns due to either partner not giving priority and encouragement to each other. Decide who is going to receive your utmost attention and follow through. This will mean you will have to stop feeding your ego and a Me First mentality. Take the lead even if other party is not approaching you first. With your initiative to bring restructure into your marriage, life may start to change in your partner too. When you bring that priority change into your approach, you will soon find emotional healing and peace. Similarly, if you are struggling with your finances, you need to prioritize your budget. Severe financial turmoil is due to lack of financial integrity and discipline.

Respecting Your Objectives and Dreams. When you are honest with yourself, have implemented integrity into your character and personality, exercise self-discipline, and you have started to take responsibility and prioritize, you will then need to learn to respect your objectives—and not forget your dreams. If you do not respect your goals, dreams, and ambitions, you will soon fall into the trap of an overwhelming situation and open yourself to people who can manipulate your thinking and behavior.

COMMON THINKING ERRORS AND HOW TO MANAGE THEM

There are ten forms or types of self-defeating thoughts. They are also referred to as cognitive distortions. This is where the real battle begins and where you can be defeated in your mind by your worst enemy—you.

Before I describe common cognitive errors and some practical strategies, I would like you to keep your notebook ready and as you go along this list, try to write your own thoughts down. It does not matter how rigid your thoughts may appear—I can assure you that once you have taken the step to defeat your negative mind-set, you will be completely set free and will be a new person. Once you have finished writing your thoughts, please sit down in a quiet place and think about ways to overcome or find alternate ways to stop your negative thought patterns. Remember that this is like your autobiography, no matter how nasty and disappointing it looks initially, in the end you will have the power to change it. These are common thinking errors:

1. Overgeneralization. How we think can have profound influence on our moods. It can also change our perception of reality because, in a way, the world is a reflection of our thinking. Our mental lens can color how we see the world. When events in life don't go our way, we can become self-critical with negative inner chatter to the point of creating negative beliefs about ourselves. We take a negative event and it becomes a pattern in our lives. We naturally relate new experiences to our old ones. So we commonly generalize based on our past experiences. Over-generalizations also make up many of our stereotypes of other people. It's like thinking of something that happened before and assuming that it will always happen again—"I always screw up." You need to recognize that *the past does not create the future*.

The language people use who tend to overgeneralize is in absolute terms including: never, always, everyone, and no one. If you find yourself using these terms frequently, then the chances are you may be vulnerable to this type of thinking. Many people who overgeneralize will have following common themes running throughout their lives:

> *"I'm a failure":* This statement assumes a permanent state of failure-hood through attaching a permanent label of failure to self. It is one that is constant and cannot change. It also discounts any success in life, so that the person can't take pride in any achievement. It also projects failure into the future. Fear of failure can keep a person from trying new things. Rather than focusing on failure or success, a better focus is to enjoy activities for their own pleasure. Carefully consider the labels you put on yourself.

> *"I never do things right":* People who tend to think this way are already disregarding what they can actually do successfully. Perhaps due to one mistake they come to a final conclusion that they can never do anything right. Don't assign a blanket statement at the start for every situation.

➤ *"Nothing ever works out for me":* These people are stuck in a rut who say and think this way. They firmly believe that nothing ever works for them. This thought then becomes part and parcel of their everyday vocabulary and they can project this into their daily life. Be careful what you say and think—always accept positive thoughts and push negative overgeneralizations out of your mind.

Overgeneralization is a false mirror. When something unpleasant or bad happens, don't look into this mirror. It will only make your problems worse. Go ahead and destroy this mirror. You need to stop and reflect on your thinking. You need to rationalize and try to look above and beyond your negative theme. You need to write down a list of overgeneralizations you have made, and see if they can be interpreted in a different way. Remember that problems are not going to go away just by focusing on the problem and feeding the problem with your junk-thinking pattern. Remember that negative thoughts are like a boomerang, they will come back into your mind.

However, when you start to force feed your negative thoughts with more positive and constructive thought, you can prove yourself wrong by actively doing something about it. Talk back to your thoughts and tell them, "I am *not* a failure." When you drip feed your mind that you are not a failure, slowly and surely you will see the results. Don't just eliminate your cognitive distortions. Go to the next level and fill your mind with positive things.

2. Catastrophizing. Catastrophizing is the hallmark of an anxious person. Catastrophizing is an irrational thought a lot of us have in believing that something is far worse than it actually is. Catastrophizing is when you start to worry and it gets out of control, because one thing leads to another, until in the end, you have your head in your hands, or you are under the duvet cover, and no persuasion from anyone will get you out. You are almost on the edge of a breakdown. You are overwhelmed, yet you did it to yourself. Therefore, when you are catastrophizing, your mind is like a floodgate of anxiety provoking thoughts that enter your mind non-stop, and you have no control over these anxious floodgates. However, you still have the ability to close these gates, and I will talk about that a bit later. This type of thinking makes dire predictions and always thinks the worst thing will happen. This illogical reasoning blows molehills into mountains without sufficient evidence.

There are two types of catastrophic reactions you can go through. First, you make a catastrophe out of a situation. For example, you're driving down the highway and a red flashing symbol pops up on the dashboard. You immediately think, "Oh my gosh, I don't have the money to fix my engine, and it may cause me to crash the car." You catastrophize in your mind about likely possible outcomes without thinking otherwise. The second type of catastrophic reaction takes you a step further. For example, you may add onto the first statement that not only is your week has been totally messed up, you will have to work overtime to pay for your broken down, hunk-a-junk car, and you may have to take the time to arrange and pay for a rental car—overall, your life stinks! It always does, your life and your car are cursed, you are forever doomed, and there isn't anything that can help things get better! So you basically take the first step, give it a global twist, and sprinkle in some future thoughts—that your life will always stink and you are cursed with cars! Catastrophic thinking, in fact, can be a trigger for panic attacks. These "what if" thoughts tend to lead from one to another until multiple fearful thoughts are all happening at once, which you could properly refer to as the snowball effect. Your thoughts gain momentum and loom larger and scarier as they increase during anxiety states.

So what are you going to do about your irrational worries and catastrophic thought life? First and foremost, you need to acknowledge the fact that you may be catastrophizing. When you think about it, these types of thoughts can actually be humorous and you might even add a little humor to them yourself, as they begin happening! For example, if you have a fear of losing control, add to that thought the idea of climbing a tree and hanging from a limb, upside down by your legs. This might sound like a ridiculous method but it can be as effective as any other method in diverting your thoughts and getting them more under your control. Second, you must write your thoughts down. Once you have written them in a notebook, have a second look at it and try to visualize any other possible way around this negative catastrophic thinking. As you continue to write your catastrophic thought pattern, you will eventually see what situations you tend to catastrophize. Now that you can see some of the direct cause and effects of your thoughts, you can work to change them.

You must challenge your catastrophic thoughts. You may need to speak to a close friend, partner, or someone you trust—ensuring that the other person is not full of anxiety—and discuss alternative rational thoughts for the situation. When you seriously practice these techniques, you will overcome.

3. Mind Reading. Mind reading is when a person will have negatively toned inferences about the thoughts, intentions, or motives of another person. For example, you are in a meeting and you start to think that your boss is talking about the company's sickness record because you took a couple of sick leave days last year. Conclusion-jumpers can often fall prey to mind reading (they believe they know the true intentions of others without talking to them) and fortune telling (predicting how things will turn out in the future and believing these predictions to be true).

You may believe that the person you are talking to is deliberately trying to ask you too many questions to find out a hidden motive when, as a matter of fact, it's just a friendly chat. You tend to exaggerate about the person and draw conclusions without having any substantial evidence. You create a mental picture, and you tend to rely on this mental picture to create dysfunctional assumptions. These dysfunctional assumptions provoke anxiety thoughts in you and will create misunderstanding and paranoid projections.

Therefore, in order to be set free from these premature assumptions, you need to admit to yourself that you have a problem of judging others quickly as well as thinking negatively about any given situation. You may have to think about alternative explanations to understand the motives of the other person. Unless you force your mind to think differently, you will remain under the grips of premature conclusion about everyone and every situation. The fact is that no one is going to come up to you to tell you what they are thinking until they decide or choose to do so.

4. Rigid Thinking—All or Nothing. People who have rigid thinking are those who see things in black and white. If your performance falls short of perfect, you see yourself as a total failure. You place people or situations in either-or categories, with no shades of gray or allowing for the complexity of most people and situations. The assertion that there is no alternative is an example of the false dichotomy taken to its ultimate extreme, in which the alternatives are reduced to one—yours. Of course you don't believe there are no alternatives, otherwise you would not bother to argue the point; rather, you oppose the alternatives and seek to dismiss them by denying their existence.

Good mirrors give true reflections. Distorted mirrors give distorted reflections and can't be trusted. When negative and depressing emotions poke up their ugly heads, it's time to check out the mirrors in your mind. It's impossible to enjoy the challenges you face when all-or-nothing thinking is in control. All-or-nothing thinking makes you feel as if you are either a total success or total failure.

What are your most common all-or-nothing thoughts? Tune in to your internal running commentary (see Challenging Depressed Thinking), and write a list of common thoughts. You also need to find the middle ground. For example on one extreme end, you think of yourself as a total failure, and on the other end you think of yourself as having to be perfect—there is no middle ground. A possible middle ground is for you to say, "I am reasonably good at this or that." List at least three different perspectives on the issue. Challenge yourself to think of even more perspectives. You don't have to believe them, just remind yourself that there are multiple ways of viewing everything. Expose yourself to other views that don't necessarily fit in with your own and see if you can find common ground. *Everything you do counts and is important.* Your life isn't measured in black and white. Go ahead and destroy this mirror so that all-or-nothing thinking never again controls your life.

5. Emotional Reasoning. The emotional reasoning mirror is about backward thinking. Its reflection tells you that you are what you feel. The facts don't matter; feelings count. If the facts contradict your feelings, then you go with your feelings and ignore the facts. In this erroneous thought life, you decide on the basis of your emotions, no matter what they are. When a person experiences unhelpful emotion (depression and anxiety), it is usually preceded by a number of unhelpful self-statements or thoughts. The basic assumption behind emotional reasoning is "Where there's smoke, there's fire." The person who acts out on emotional reasoning is also perhaps displaying his or her insecurity and creates a self-fulfilling prophecy of failure. With emotional reasoning, you are constantly amplifying your thinking to generate high voltage thoughts emerging from your weak brain that destroys your self-esteem, confidence, assertiveness, and judgment.

God designed you to think with your head and feel with your heart, and as long as you do it that way, you won't have a problem with emotional reasoning. Thinking with your heart is certainly a risky business and can lead to failure. You have to remember that in emotional reasoning, your feelings or emotions are taking you for rough ride with turbulence all the way through the journey. Even if you try to land somewhere, high possibility is you will crash land and this can cause damage to your land of emotion. You really need to sow in the garden of your emotion a well balanced and rational thoughts which in due season will produce a harvest of stable and best possible emotional response. Think twice before you allow your feelings to change into monster. Once you unleash the monster from your emotion, the only outcome would be disaster. Emotional reasoning is a tough mirror to deal with because it's human nature to think with your heart. The truth is, it's acceptable to think with your heart as long as it doesn't get into the driver's seat and assume control.

6. Blaming. When we blame, we hold other people responsible for our pain or take the other track and blame ourselves for every problem. I have seen many marital relationships break down because too much blame game is being played by the couples. You know you are not accepting personal responsibility if you blame others for your problems, life situation, hardships, character flaws, and just about everything and anything else that is wrong in your life. Or rather than accepting the blame or responsibility for your life, you make excuses. Everything and anybody is to blame—except you.

Two useful quotes I found are so true:

> The best years of your life are the ones in which you decide **your problems are your own.** You do not blame them on your mother, the ecology, or the president. You realize that **you control your own destiny.**
>
> *–Albert Ellis*[5]

> All blame is a **waste of time.** No matter how much fault you find with another, and regardless of how much you blame him, it **will not change you.** The only thing blame does is to keep the focus off you when you are looking for external reasons to explain **your unhappiness or frustration.** You may succeed in making another feel guilty about something by blaming him,

but you won't succeed in changing whatever it is about you
that is making you unhappy.

–*Wayne Dyer*[6]

I suppose sometimes people find it enjoyable to blame and criticize others. They waste their energies and time finding fault without realizing that they are out of tune themselves. They may project their feelings and emotions onto someone else and try to find an escape route to let go of their emotions or perhaps inferiority complex. Hence, they find it easier to blame others. *Two things are hard for the heart: running up stairs and running down people.*

Projection is a common defense mechanism where people get upset with a trait in someone else that they wish to deny in themselves. They suppress the knowledge that they have the same trait and externalize blame on the other person. They are highly sensitized to the unwanted behaviors in others and transfer their horror and anger at their own unwanted inner trait to an outside person. Much of their internal thoughts or words during an argument is focused on blaming the other person. We all have a bit of projection in us, but some people have the need to blame others big time, thus obstructing their own growth and learning. People who project blame often feel a hidden stigma and shame at possessing a disgraceful personality trait so they "project" or transfer anger onto others to distract themselves from knowing the truth about their own self. They become so highly sensitized to the presence of their unwanted traits that it interferes with their social informational processing. They don't see reality as it is and then operate out of their misperceptions. How do you know if you are projecting your anger onto others? Preoccupation, judgments, and anger about others' behavior are projection. If you spot it, you got it!

Therefore, you need to make the decision to change. Look into your personal life and also your past hurts. If you are carrying clutter from the past, make sure you start to deal with it head-on rather than projecting your clutter onto someone else. You need to now let go of the blame and resentment you have been carrying all these years. You may perhaps have to speak it out loud to release people from the prison of blame.

7. **Filtering and Magnifying.** Filtering and magnifying is when we take negative details and magnify them while filtering out all positive

aspects of a situation. Ten things can go right, but a person operating under the influence of a mental filter may only notice the one thing that went wrong. (Add a little overgeneralization and all-or-nothing thinking to the equation, and you have a recipe for major stress.) The Law of Focus states that what you focus on expands into your mind and then into your life. Because negative thinking has a negative focus, it magnifies everything that's negative. Conversely, when you don't focus on positive things, they fade from your heart and mind. This is just another way negative operating systems wreak havoc in your mind. An unremitting negative focus causes negative images to expand on the motion picture screen of your mind. Negative events become bigger and bigger until they are larger than life, and they are the only things you can see.

This person filters out all the good things that life has and focuses only on the negative parts of life. You pick on a single negative detail and dwell on it. You overly dwell on the negative and totally ignore the positives. You may make predictions about what will happen in the future based on little information. In magnifying/minimizing, you blow things out of proportion. You tend to minimize the strengths and qualities of yourself and others and magnify and exaggerate the supposed weaknesses, mistakes, and errors. Stop and take the time to concentrate on the things that went right, the plans that worked out, the relationships you have, the people who love you. Make a list of all the good things in your life. Keep this list somewhere you can see it—and add to it as you realize and discover all of the many blessings you have.

8. Always Being Right. If you are caught in the trap of always wanting to be right, please x-ray your emotions to see the defects in this kind of thinking pattern. Even if you are provided with possible explanation proving that you may not be right, you just can't accept the fact that you could ever be wrong. You are not willing to bend or be flexible. You put on a sarcastic front and possibly start to live in a land of your own where the ground you are standing on will sooner or later suffer an earthquake. You try to portray yourself to be Mr. or Ms. Right. No fault could ever be found in you, and you are just naturally very gifted in the art of false self-claim of being right.

Self-righteousness is a self-destructive path toward a collision course with yourself—one day you will just fall apart. Therefore, it is essential that you respect other points of view, and when someone tells you something contrary to your belief, you must with humbleness accept that and become a good listener. This will gain you respect in your relationships and your work.

9. Making "Should" Statements. People who say "should" all the time have a list of ironclad rules about how they and others "should" behave. People who break the rules make them angry, and they feel guilty when they violate these rules. These people may often believe they are trying to motivate themselves with shoulds and shouldn'ts, as if they have to be punished before they can do anything. These people concentrate on what they think should or ought to be rather than the actual situation they are faced with. They have rigid rules that they think should always apply no matter what the circumstances. This also creates and leads to other cognitive distortions such as self-righteousness. Try replacing *should* with some flexibility of may.

10. Jumping to Conclusions. When a negative mind comes under pressure, it starts acting as if it has special powers that enable it to predict the future and even see into the minds of other people. Do you find that you are very impatient and tend to quickly jump to conclusions about any given situation or circumstances? If you examine the ability of the negative mind to look into the future and to read the thoughts of other people, you will not be impressed with its track record. A negative mind does an excellent job of jumping to conclusions, and those conclusions are consistently negative and wrong. Jumping to conclusions and mind reading have never worked in the past, don't work in the present, and will not work in the future. Don't waste your time jumping to conclusions or attempting to read the minds of other people. Smash, bash, and trash this mirror and make your life better today.

ENDNOTES

1. http://www.brainyquote.com/quotes/authors/d/denis _waitley_3.html; accessed May 4, 2010.

2. http://www.brainyquote.com/quotes/authors/m/martin _luther_king_jr_5.html; accessed May 4, 2010.

3. http://www.brainyquote.com/quotes/authors/m/martin_luther_king_jr_5.html; accessed May 4, 2010.

4. http://www.brainyquote.com/quotes/authors/a/albert_einstein_8.html; accessed May 4, 2010.

5. http://www.brainyquote.com/quotes/authors/a/albert_ellis.html; accessed May 4, 2010.

6. http://www.achieving-life-abundance.com/quotes-by-wayne-dyer.html; accessed May 13, 2010.

Chapter 7

Negating Negative Emotions and Possessing a Positive Mind

By now you should be able to identify your negative emotions and particularly negative automatic thoughts (NAT). You are now aware of how your negative thoughts have the power to twist the truth in your mind to feed you with fear, anxiety, depression, low self-esteem, low confidence, and problems like these. And you also know by now that you can control your NATs. Experiencing such emotions from time to time is OK; however, if you are frequently experiencing these harmful negative thoughts, the likelihood is that your thinking pattern is faulty.

Negative thoughts reveal what's happening inside your mind. They reflect your approach to life and your habits of thought. Some people run their minds in such a manner that negative thoughts are rarely present. Other people find a continual cascade of negative thoughts rushing through their minds.

Emotions that can become negative are hate, anger, jealousy, and sadness. Negative emotions can dampen our enthusiasm for life, depending on how long we let them affect us and the way we choose to express them. Negative emotions stop us from thinking and behaving rationally and seeing situations in their true perspective. When this occurs, we tend to see only what we want to see and remember only what we want to remember. This prolongs the anger or grief and prevents us from enjoying life.

Our emotions are important to our overall well-being. They help us in decision making, predicting behavior, survival, boundary setting, communication, happiness, and creating unity. However, negative emotions can cripple us in all domains of our lives.

One of the remarkable discoveries of the twentieth century was the existence of black holes. The density of matter in a black hole is massive beyond description. Black holes possess such an immense gravitational field not even light can escape its grasp. It literally pulls all matter and light into its center. If you went near a black hole, you would disappear completely without a trace.

Negativity is the black hole of the mind. If you spend time thinking negative thoughts, your life slowly disappears into a black hole. Negative thinking is unimaginably powerful. The only safe way to escape the black hole of negativity is to say NO to this destructive emotion.

Often we allow people into our lives who treat us as we expect to be treated. If we are willing to tolerate negative treatment from others, or treat others in negative ways, it is possible that we also treat ourselves similarly. If you are an abuser or a recipient, seriously consider how you treat yourself. What sorts of things do you say to yourself? Do thoughts such as "I'm stupid" or "I never do anything right" dominate your thinking? Learning to love and care for yourself increases self-esteem and makes it more likely that you will have healthy, intimate relationships.

All of our negative emotions have some positive value. In the proper amount, each negative feeling helps us stay on course toward health and happiness. They do this by telling us when we are veering away from our:

- Goals.
- Values.
- Beliefs.
- Standards.
- Comfort zones.
- Physical health.
- Happiness.

If we had no fear, no regrets, no guilt, and no sadness, we would be little more than unfeeling, uncaring robots. But since we are humans, we do have feelings, and the more human we are, the more ability we have to experience feelings—positive as well as negative. Let's see what we can learn from a few common negative feelings.

Fear. In the proper amount, fear protects us. It protects us from both physical and psychological danger. In excessive amounts, however, it paralyzes us or distorts our perception of reality.

Anger. In many ways, anger is an expression of fear. For example, when man was living in caves and fighting off predators, fear quickly became anger, and was an important survival response. When he was physically threatened, his anger helped him to either attack or frighten away his predators. In other words, anger empowers us to help control a threatening situation. Nowadays the threats are more often psychological than physical (though it seems that trend is reversing with the increase in violence and terrorism). In other words, we primarily use anger to protect our egos, not our physical safety.

Disappointments. Disappointment is something we cause ourselves. It arises out of our expectations. It is based on how we think the world should be and how we think people should act. When things don't go the way we expect them to, it simply means that our interpretation of reality was faulty. It tells us that we don't understand reality as well as we thought we did—our expectations were unrealistic. A more intense form of disappointment is bitterness, which tells us that not only did we expect something, but we started to count on it or depend on it.

Guilt. When you feel guilty, you are at war with yourself. This is a good time to examine your standards, apologize, ask for forgiveness, make restitution, learn from the experience, and learn to forgive yourself.

Evaluate Your Standards. Ask yourself if the standards you are comparing your actions against are really your standards. In other words, did you consciously select them, or were they just handed down to you or forced upon you (as is the case with most religion-based guilt)? If you do not really believe in the standard, you are punishing yourself needlessly.

Feeling Overwhelmed. When we feel overwhelmed, it is sign that we are trying to tackle too much. During such times, the well-balanced person is able to step back and sort out the facts and their feelings. When we feel overwhelmed there are always other feelings involved, and fear is one of them.

Feeling Uncomfortable. When you feel uncomfortable, you often actually feel it in your body, usually your stomach. Thus the term *gut instincts*. Your body is trying to tell you to watch out, be careful, or to take some action to get out of a situation. When you feel uncomfortable, use your upper brain to analyze the situation. Determine what is making you feel uncomfortable. Chances are, there are several specific negative feelings. Identifying them helps you determine what action is necessary. For example, you may think you cannot get out of your financial turmoil, but there *are* rational ways.

Negative thoughts create personal inertia; you become stuck where you are. The paralysis of negative thinking makes constructive action extremely difficult. Negative thinking creates the fear of making a mistake. The possible negative consequences of failure makes you stagnant. There are people who live in a habitually negative state. These are the pessimists. People living in this state have a Ph.D. in pessimism; it's their specialty. They are experts at filling their minds with pessimistic thoughts; it's their way of life and their way of looking at the world. They have fully assimilated all of the negative programming encountered during their lifetime. Pessimistic thinking isn't something they do only when they are fatigued or in a state of overload. They do it all the time. Their cup of life is always half empty rather than half full. It's hard to turn a pessimist into an optimist, because they need a mind transplant. They need total mind reprogramming. Pessimism works for them, and they really don't want to change. Although they may not enjoy their lives as much as an optimist, their comfort zone easily accommodates their pessimistic worldview.

Toxic waste consists of words, thoughts, sounds, images, and emotions that are harmful. They damage your heart and mind and make it more difficult to live as a positive person. Toxic waste forms the heart and soul of cognitive distortions.

Well you may ask that after so many years of hurt, disappointments, breakdown in relationships, etc., how can I be positive? You enter a training ground to win your battle over your negative thoughts and change them—force them into positive thoughts. This will require a lot of effort on your part. You need to install positive software in you to reap the benefits of being positive. A positive mind is not an accident. It's something you do on purpose. A persistently positive focus creates a consistently positive mind.

The focus of your mind is critical. Focus selects the programs running in your mind. When you are negative and focused on everything wrong, your mind runs programs that confirm and reinforce those beliefs. When your focus is positive, your mind runs programs that confirm and reinforce your positive thoughts.

POSSESS A POSITIVE MIND

The war for a positive mind is fought on the battlefield of focus. When you control your focus, you control your thoughts and emotions. A positive focus pushes your heart and mind in a positive direction. A positive focus gives you powerful leverage over your mind and will help you to control it. When you focus on a thought, it forces your mind to look in the direction of that thought. When you focus on it for a minute, you push your mind in that direction for a minute. When you consistently focus on it for weeks and months, your life will become habitually positive.

Characteristics of a positive mind:

1. A positive mind has a positive focus.

2. A positive mind interprets events in an optimistic manner, giving them a positive meaning. It takes bad things and makes them into something better.

3. A positive mind looks for the good in every situation.

4. A positive mind has positive expectations.

5. A positive mind is positively congruent and your inner being will move in a positive direction.

6. A positive mind manifests a positive spirituality based on love.

7. A positive mind has a positive self-image and self-esteem.

You are the one who chooses the meaning of what happens in your life. Each event is devoid of meaning until you make a decision what it means to you. Your choice determines if your problems are catastrophes or opportunities for growth. A positive mind is enabling; it empowers you to say

The first time you say yes, a small positive change happens. .ime you say yes, the positive change becomes bigger.

people say yes to life so infrequently that positive change never has a chance to compound and work its magic. This is unfortunate because the best things in life happen when you ride the exponential curve of positive change all the way to the top.

Just eliminating your negative thoughts does not make you a positive person. You need to make a constant effort to fuel your mind with positive thoughts. You need to talk, read, write, look, and listen to positive things in your life. If you do these things, a tidal wave of positive thoughts will sweep through your heart and mind, and it won't be long before a positive mind-set is up and running. Your mind will be more controlled and focused. There are no more tsunamis in your mind.

You may also need to look into negatives in your life. Start being an assertive person and claim the positive feed into your life. It is going to change and is bound to change. Start your day by writing the first thought that comes to your mind. You need to closely monitor your thought life every day. At the end of the day, I want you to sit down with your notebook and look into all the negatives and positives and count them. See which is high in number. You need to trash your negative thoughts with positive thoughts. Either do your research or ask a family or friend to help. The more you practice this technique, you will see that your life course is set for onward and upward journey. You will not be static.

Remember, negative thoughts are like parasites. Focusing on them is like giving them a transfusion with your own blood. You become psychologically anemic as they suck the blood from your mental veins. They become stronger as you become weaker. You destroy yourself when you think negatively.

When negative thoughts pop into your mind, they are weak and vulnerable. If you don't infuse them with your energy, they die. They cannot attack and suck the energy from your mind by themselves. They wait for you to do the job for them. The energy transfer begins only if you focus on them. Do not argue with your negative thoughts. The more you argue with them, the more they will argue back to prove their case. Very soon it will turn into a court room battle. Remember, you are the judge and the jury. You give the verdict to your negative thoughts.

BECOME A POSITIVE PERSON

The following are proven successful ways to become a positive person.

Practice positive affirmations. Remind yourself that you are not a failure. You can achieve balance in your relationships. You will reach your goal. Speak these thoughts aloud to confirm your commitment and belief in yourself.

Start using positive words in your daily vocabulary. Negative thoughts will continually attack you; however, you do not have to give in to these negative thoughts, and you can be assertive and talk back to your negative thoughts.

Learn to direct your thoughts. This technique, used by psychotherapists, can help you to control your thoughts when you start to feel down or anxious. Create a happy thought, a positive image, or give yourself positive feedback to keep bad feelings in check.

Learn to analyze the situation that may be provoking negative thoughts in your mind. Reflect on the situation and use problems as learning opportunities—analyze how successfully you have dealt with it.

The past is behind you, and no matter how badly things went, you cannot change your past. Whenever you feel negative thoughts about the past, replace them immediately with positive thoughts about the future. This is another area where many face their defeats and give up. Make sure you move forward and focus on now and here. Focus on what you can do today in order to have *better tomorrow*. Do not look back into the alleyways of your past that will create negative automatic thoughts and cause stagnation in your life.

Associate with positive-thinking people. Positivity is contagious, so surround yourself with friends and family members who look on the bright side. I am not saying not to talk to family members who always are negative, but be careful that you do not pull yourself down in their negative conversations. Try doing something nice for someone you care about.

Distract yourself from your negative feelings by embracing your sense of adventure. Check out part of town you have never been to or just spend time reliving the happy memories from things around your home.

Practice relaxation techniques with soothing music playing in the background. Buy or rent relaxation CDs widely available in major bookstores and music shops.

When you are faced with a challenge, look into the heart of the challenge for a solution in the challenge itself.

Change your attitude. Have an attitude of gratitude as this helps you conquer any challenge.

Don't wallow in your problems. Instead, work toward finding a solution and resolution. You'll feel proactive and in control of your life.

Create realistic goals. Make your objectives attainable, and don't frustrate yourself by unrealistic targets.

Don't feel defeated, and make positive thinking a habit. Don't just practice thinking positively when you are feeling down; make it a habit to practice being positive in any weather.

Overcoming Depression and Anxiety

Overcoming depression is hard, perhaps the hardest thing you will ever do. Fighting against depression isn't a stroll in the park—it's a dogfight. But if you decide to join the fray, you can win the battle and drive depression from your mind. If you want to have a mind free from depression, nobody can stop you.

You cannot overcome depression or anxious thoughts just by sitting in your lounge chair and doing nothing about it. You need to take the first step to deliverance from your negative thoughts or everything will remain static. Now that you recognize your negative automatic thoughts and you know what your weak areas are in your personality, which is making you more vulnerable, you have to replace negative thoughts with more rational and appropriate alternative interpretations of situations. Most individuals who are not depressed, maintain relatively positive core beliefs—"I can do most things competently," compared with "I am inadequate," which is typical of people with depression. Therefore, recognition of cognitive errors and cognitive restructuring involves active participation in the process.

If you are depressed, you can most likely see this negative pattern of thinking in yourself. To accomplish successful depression self-help, you have to change your pattern of thinking. As Dr. Aaron T. Beck wrote in 1976, "The underlying attitude, however, is the component that needs to be changed ultimately if the totality of the depression is to be influenced. Thus, the goal is *cognitive modification.*"[1] The Beck cognitive triad (1. My future is hopeless, 2. I am inadequate, 3. All I do results in failure—self, world, future) is active in most individuals with depression and all the three domains on this triad will have its own negative automatic thoughts. Individuals who suffer from depression will have a bleak view of self, the world/environment, and future.

Therefore, in depression there are three questions you need to consider and try to answer:

> ➤ What is the evidence for these thoughts?

> ➤ Is there another way of looking at this?

> ➤ Would it be better to look at this in a different way?

When you answer these questions, you are on your way to overcoming depression and eliminating negative emotions from your mind.

You can beat negative emotions in a step-by-step manner by:

1. Distracting yourself from negative thoughts.

2. Challenging cognitive distortions by keeping a thought diary.

3. Problem-solving techniques.

1. Distraction Techniques: When you are feeling very anxious or tense, thoughts and worries can whirl around in your head, making you feel even worse. As soon as you are faced with intense negative emotions that are driving your depression and anxiety, it is sometimes good to divert your thinking in a different direction. Many well-meaning therapists and self-help books recommend using distraction techniques such as keeping busy, counting backward from 100, snapping a rubber band on your wrist, reading a book, doing puzzles, etc., as methods to alleviate anxiety and negative thoughts. You may also find it useful to perhaps use relaxation techniques, for example, playing some soothing music, deep breathing techniques, meditation, etc. It may be beneficial to talk to a family member or friend. Concentrating your mind on simple exercises such as mental arithmetic, reciting the lyrics of a song, working on a word-search or simple crossword can be very effective at taking your mind off your worries and reducing anxiety.

Focusing your mind on the world around you can effectively distract you from your worries. You could try describing the view outside the window as accurately as possible, as if trying to describe it to someone who is not there. Alternatively, describe an object in the room in great detail. Try counting the bricks in a wall or the different colors in a painting. If you are walking down the street, try focusing on the people around you—look for people wearing red jackets, with curly hair, or beards. Try inventing stories about the people you see—what might their lives be like, what jobs might they have? Alternatively, focus on what you see in the shop windows or on passing vehicles.

Being active is a great way of reducing anxiety. Activity distracts you from your worries and can also reduce some of the physical tension and stress that builds up when anxious. Being physically active such as going for a walk or a bike ride, going swimming, doing some gardening, or going dancing are all great ways to reduce anxiety. It is often also helpful to carry out your normal, day-to-day jobs or chores. For example, cleaning the car, ironing, washing, or even vacuuming the house can all take your mind off unpleasant thoughts and worries. Spending time with others is a very effective way of distracting yourself and is important for building relationships with others. This could involve phoning a friend or relative, talking or playing with your children, going out for coffee with a friend, or making time to talk to your partner about their day.

2. Challenging cognitive distortions: Everyone says negative things to themselves. There are various types of talk and they all need to be challenged. It's very hard work challenging negative thoughts, especially when we're depressed, but it will help. This is where your mood diary is useful. Once a negative and challenging thought enters your mind, talk directly to that particular thought and try to see other side of the situation. When you challenge negative thoughts, ask yourself: Is enough evidence to come to this conclusion? Are there any gaps in my thinking?

➤ Train yourself to be more aware of what you are saying to yourself when you are feeling bad.

➤ Learn to test the reasonableness of your negative thoughts.

➤ You will still feel sad and disappointed when things go wrong and it's important to experience these feelings. Our aim is to stop this from developing into depression, not to cut out the normal ups and downs of life.

If you are struggling with the fear that something bad is going to happen to you, you may have to ask yourself: What are the realistic chances this will happen to me? Have I underestimated my own ability to deal with the difficulty? You will very soon realize that by practicing these simple challenges, you will become more confident in dealing with the problem and particularly coping with it.

Other question to ask yourself:

➤ Is this situation as bad as I am making out to be?

➤ What is the worst thing that could happen? How likely is it?

➤ What is the best thing that could happen?

➤ What is most likely to happen?

➤ Is there anything good about this situation?

➤ Will this matter five years from now?

When you feel anxious, depressed, or stressed-out, your self-talk is likely to become extreme. You may be more likely to expect the worst and focus on the most negative aspects of your situation. So, it's helpful to try and put things into their proper perspective. Recognizing that your current way of thinking might be self-defeating (doesn't make you feel good or help you to get what you want), can sometimes motivate you to look at things from a different perspective. If you have negative or critical thoughts, have a go at challenging them. Once you get into the habit of disputing your negative self-talk, you'll find it easier to handle difficult situations, and as a result, you'll feel less stressed and more confident and in control.

3. Problem-Solving Techniques: Problem-solving techniques help you adjust your mind-set to a different level. You can empower yourself, feel confident about yourself and your relationships, and it will increase your confidence and self-esteem. Everyone experiences difficulties at some time or another—that's part of life. In fact, many psychologists would argue that facing and overcoming life's challenges is essential if we are to develop into strong, mentally healthy people. Put simply "having problems is no problem." The trick is to learn how to deal with our problems and challenges effectively and efficiently.

First and foremost, you need to define your problem and or your negative thoughts. As mentioned previously, when you have identified negative emotion and challenged it, you are now ready to think in a different way to resolve the problem, which may be contributing to your negative thinking.

Second, you need to understand the difference between feelings and facts. Feelings can be changed. However, facts cannot be changed. If you are trying to change the facts, you are heading on toward a collision with frustration. Therefore, you have to accept the facts and tell yourself to move on. For example, you may be feeling very distressed and catastrophic about your financial situation, which now is at the verge of bankruptcy. You can certainly change and modify your feelings and accept that bankruptcy is a fact.

Set goals and try to determine the outcome of any given problem or a situation. Make few assumptions and perhaps it may make some sense to discuss these possible outcomes with a trusted friend or family member.

Now you are ready to narrow down some of the options that you have generated in the previous step. It is important that you examine each of the options, and think about how realistic each is, how likely you would be to implement that solution, and the potential drawbacks of each. For example, if your solution costs a great deal of money or requires many hours of effort each day, this may be too difficult to implement. As you start to narrow down your choices, remember, no problem solution is perfect and all will have drawbacks, but you can always revise the solution if it does not work the way you want it to work.

Once you have examined all your options and decided on one that seems to accomplish your goals and minimizes the costs, it is time to test it. Make sure that when you implement this solution, you do so wholeheartedly and give it your best effort. During this stage, you should continue to examine the chosen solution and the degree to which it is "solving" your problem. If you find that the solution is too hard to implement or it is just not working, revise it or try something else. Trying to solve these problems is never an easy task, and it may take several solutions before something works. But *don't give up hope*, because with persistence and your best effort, many difficult decisions and problems can be made better!

BEHAVIOR MODIFICATION

Behavior modification is used to treat a variety of problems in both adults and children. Behavior modification has been successfully used to treat *obsessive-compulsive disorder* (OCD), *attention-deficit/hyperactivity disorder* (ADHD), phobias, enuresis (bed-wetting), generalized anxiety disorder, separation anxiety disorder, and depressive negative cognitions.

The goals of behavior therapy or modification are:

➤ Improve daily functioning.

➤ Reduce emotional distress.

➤ Enhance your relationships.

➤ Maximize your potential.

With behavior modification, you can develop a new behavior, strengthen existing behavior, stop inappropriate behavior, and modify emotional behavior.

Modern behavioral-cognitive psychotherapy can be used in the treatment of a large number of conditions. The emphasis on cognitive or behavior aspects of therapy can vary depending on the issue. For example, the emphasis may be more toward cognitive therapy when treating depression, or the emphasis may be more toward behavior therapy when treating obsessive-compulsive disorder.

COPING WITH ANXIETY

Anxiety is the feeling we get when our body responds to a frightening or threatening experience. It has been called the fight or flight response and is simply your body preparing for action either to fight danger or run away from it as fast as possible. The purpose of the physical symptoms of anxiety, therefore, is to prepare your body to cope with threat. To understand what is happening in your body, imagine that you are about to be attacked. As soon as you are aware of the threat, your muscles tense ready for action. Your heart beats faster to carry blood to your muscles and brain where it is most needed. You breathe faster to provide oxygen, which is needed for energy. You sweat to stop your body from overheating. Your mouth becomes dry and your tummy may have butterflies. When you realize that the "attacker" is in fact a friend, the feelings die away, but you may feel shaky and weak after the experience.

Here are some suggestions you can implement in your daily life if you are suffering from anxiety and panic symptoms:

➤ *Perform deep-breathing exercises to relax your mind and calm your body.* Breathe with the use of your muscles located around the belly. Try focusing on your belly as it rises when you inhale. Do this five to eight times to reduce anxiety.

➤ *If you feel that anxiety is rising, move your body.* Cool your head, take a walk, exercise, or engage in any form of physical activity. Doing this will let your body release toxic body chemicals and give you relief.

➤ *Anxiety is an effect of too much negativity in the atmosphere.* Practice converting anxiety into something positive. Use anxiety as something that you can benefit from. Anxiety is not to be feared but is rather a sign of what you need to do.

➤ *Manage anxiety as soon as possible.* If you feel that something is not right, correct it quickly. Don't let negativity build up inside your head; release it by solving everything that bothers you as soon as possible. Avoid getting into an all-or-nothing pattern of thinking as discussed previously.

➤ Finally, *learn to forget the past.* Anxiety can arise from past experiences such as arguments, making mistakes, not keeping a promise, and the like. Try to accept and forget the past; and concentrate more on how to avoid such things.

SELF-ESTEEM IS THE KEY

Self-esteem is your opinion of yourself. High self-esteem is a good opinion of yourself and low self-esteem is a bad opinion of yourself. Low self-esteem results from a poor self-image. Low self-esteem feeds your negative thinking and makes you believe negative comments others make. This can cause you to lose confidence—it is vital to end negative thoughts if you want to build your self-esteem.

Steps to enhance your self-esteem:

> ➤ Change negative thoughts to positive thoughts about yourself.

> ➤ Replace negative thoughts with positive ones every time you realize you are thinking negative thoughts.

> ➤ Repeat your positive thought over and over to yourself, out loud whenever possible, and even share them with another person if possible.

> ➤ Pay attention to your own needs and wants. Listen to what your body, mind, and heart are telling you. For instance, if your body is telling you that you have been sitting down too long, stand up and stretch. If your heart is longing to spend more time with a special friend, do it. If your mind is telling you to clean up your basement, listen to your favorite music, or stop thinking bad thoughts about yourself, take those thoughts seriously.

> ➤ You may be so busy, or feel so badly about yourself, that you spend little or no time doing things you enjoy—things like playing a musical instrument, doing a craft project, flying a kite, or going fishing. Make a list of things you enjoy doing. Then do something from that list every day. Add to the list anything new that you discover you enjoy doing.

> ➤ Spend time with people who make you feel good about yourself. Spend time with people who treat you well. Avoid people who treat you badly.

> ➤ Take advantage of opportunities to learn something new or improve your skills. Take a class or go to a seminar.

➤ Do something nice for another person. Smile at someone who looks sad. Say a few kind words to the check-out cashier. Help your spouse with an unpleasant chore. Take a meal to a friend who is sick. Send a card to an acquaintance. Volunteer for a worthy organization.

➤ Make signs with the positive thought, hang them in places where you see them often—like on your refrigerator door or on the mirror in your bathroom—and repeat the thought to yourself several times when you see it.

➤ Make an affirming and positive list of your strengths and abilities. Making lists, rereading them often, and rewriting them from time to time will help you feel better about yourself. If you have a journal, you can write your lists there. If you don't, any piece of paper will do.

➤ Develop a scrapbook that celebrates you and the wonderful person you are. Include pictures of yourself at different ages, writings you enjoy, mementos of things you have done and places you have been, cards you have received, etc. Or set up a place in your home that "celebrates you." Decorate the space with objects that remind you of the special person you are. If you don't have a private space that you can leave set up, put the objects in a special bag, box, or drawer and set them up in the space whenever you do this work. Take them out and look at them whenever you need to bolster your self-esteem.

BE ASSERTIVE

Being assertive is the skill of saying what we need or want, or protecting ourselves from what we do not want, while respecting the needs and rights of others. It is being able to communicate appropriately in a direct, open, and honest way. When you allow the needs, opinions, or judgment of others to become more important than your own, you may feel hurt, anxious, and even angry. This kind of behavior is often indirect, emotionally dishonest and self-denying. Assertiveness is not something that is inherited. Assertiveness is a skill that anyone can learn. Being assertive requires only one thing, your decision.

For you to be assertive, you need to know the rules of engagement. These rules are:

➤ You need to respect yourself and get to know yourself better.

➤ You recognize your own needs. Make sure you give importance to your own needs.

➤ Make clear "I" statements. For example, you may disagree with someone's decision and therefore you need to let them know that, "I disagree with your decision."

➤ You also need to allow yourself to make mistakes. You are not perfect. You can and will make mistakes. However, you need to make sure that when you make mistakes, you recognize them, rectify them, and learn from them for your own personal growth.

➤ Assertiveness involves changing your mind-set. You cannot dwell on the negatives. You need to face reality. You cannot beat around the bush.

➤ You also need to allow time to think about certain matters when people ask you for things.

➤ You need to learn to enjoy success with yourself and let others know about what you have achieved.

➤ Ask for what you want. Don't expect people to read your mind about your needs and if you don't get what you want, don't become easily miserable and sulk.

➤ You also need to recognize that you are not responsible for other people's actions that are harmful or inappropriate. Do not blame yourself. Acknowledge your shortcomings.

➤ Learn to respect other people and their rights to be assertive in return. If they are being assertive with you, do not get offended quickly or dive into misery.

➤ Learn to say no sometimes when you do not want to participate.

➤ Being assertive can save your relationships. Many relationships are ruined because partners lack the ability to state their needs and wants assertively. After all, if you never talk about what bothers you, then you will become frustrated. Your frustration will turn into aggression, and you will reach a point where you tell your partner "I can't take it anymore." Assertiveness helps you avoid problems because it prevents the accumulation of feelings that might lead to frustration.

Are You Overly Sensitive?

Over-sensitivity is being overly affected by an external influence that minimally affects most other people—for example, not being able to tolerate constructive criticism that others normally tolerate. Overly sensitive people are more likely to have bad moods, get depressed, and be moody because their mood changes with every small event that happens. An emotionally sensitive person is a fragile person, or a person labeled "handle with care." Overly sensitive people have a hard time loving people simply because they feel the pain that results from a breakup in an exaggerated way.

There are many ways that can help you deal with your over sensitivity, but most of them root to one source—changing your way of thinking and your perception of situations. Rationalize your negative thinking that is provoking you to be over-sensitive.

Deal With Your Shame

Dealing with shame requires that you understand: where shame comes from, why you sometimes feel shameful, and what the difference is between shame and guilt. Guilt is a message that notifies you that you are deviating from your values, but shame is a feeling that tells you that you may not be adequate or worthy!

Many times people find themselves complaining about their lacks, speaking of being victims, or generally expressing negative viewpoints toward themselves or the world. The more a person stays stuck in such a mental or emotional place, the more real such a state becomes in their personal world. Through the process of living, we all develop our own personal system of polarities, where something is good or bad, positive or negative, up or down. Changing negatives into positives is part of the developmental process of growing toward the higher good.

When we react instead of consciously acting, we often regret later that we could have done something in a better way. These past events often serve as anchors until you release and let go of any negative beliefs or memories of them. You may have had relationships in your past that you didn't handle the best way. There may be an old hurt, something said in anger, or a feeling of being let down or letting someone else down that is lingering in your memory. As an exercise, go back and change these negative recollections by looking at the positive gifts that people had for you, and see the good you did for them. Then transmit forgiveness and selfless love to those people at whatever age they were when you experienced them. You will heal yourself and others throughout this process.

The healing will also take place in the present time, and will erase any projection of negative patterns in your future behavior. Always remember that had it not been for those past events, you would not be who you are in the present! Keep in mind that every time you replay the words or imagery of a guilty action, it is like reliving the error again. The act of asking for forgiveness and transmitting forgiveness must also be coupled with forgiving yourself. No matter how terrible the act, there is no purpose served in self-accusation and reminding yourself of failure. Simply acknowledge the guilty action, ask God's forgiveness, forgive yourself, and get on with your growth without beating yourself up any longer. You can't change what has already happened, but your choices in the future can now be more directed. You must begin living in the here and now. Make the present perfect.

UNLOCK SELF-HEALING THOUGHTS

All doctors acknowledge the power of your mind to heal your body. They use terms to explain away such healings like the "placebo effect" or a "state of remission," but they know it's your mind that is creating such an effect on your body. Your body has a natural ability to protect and heal itself on a day-to-day basis. All so-called "cures" that take place in the world are simply stimulations of your own immune system, or a miracle healing from God. When your energy is high, so is your health. When your energy is low, so is your ability to heal itself, and it's at this time that you're most susceptible.

KEEP YOURSELF MOTIVATED

Many people rely on others to motivate them into doing something. Self-motivation is a rarer quality, and it is also a distinct leadership trait. Most people do things for a reward of some kind, but some people do things because they feel it is the right thing to do, or they feel good about doing it, or it gives them a sense of purpose. Keeping yourself motivated can sometimes be difficult. Study yourself and determine when you are the most active and effective. When are you the most inactive and ineffective? How does the time of day affect your behavior? How does the type of activity, what you ate, the type of exercise, or any particular thoughts affect your behavior? Gain as much insight about what contributes to keeping yourself motivated as possible.

People normally have a tendency to choose a path requiring less energy, unless there is a pleasurable reward they can obtain after exerting themselves. Stimulating the pleasure zone in the limbic system of the brain is one way to reward yourself. It is often called *fun*. Having fun requires a lot of energy and effort, but the reward is a broad stimulation of the senses in a pleasurable way. So always add fun to your life, especially after completing difficult tasks. Learn what stimulates you pleasurably, and create this stimulation as your reward.

BOOST YOUR SELF-CONFIDENCE

With many people, there is a distinct need to feel important. Without this feeling fulfilled, people often suffer from self-doubt, guilt, insecurity, and low self-worth. These people go to great lengths to maintain a good reputation, demonstrate that they are needed, to gain a bit of self-esteem, to prove their superiority, to show that they're right, or even to meet a challenge presented to them. If you diplomatically satisfy these areas to such ego-oriented people, you become master over any situation with them. Their emotional mind loves it, and their logical mind is suspended. Usually, the lack of self-confidence is associated with negative self-talk, which are the negative phrases and words they keep telling themselves while doing their normal thinking process. Stopping those negative words and phrases and replacing them with positive ones can not only increase confidence but can help fix many emotional problems.

Some people have developed the terrible habit of always comparing themselves to others; what's worse is that they choose to compare criteria that almost always puts them at the weak end of the comparison. They ignore all that is great about them and pick just this one thing that they lack and compare it to others. On finding that they are different, they feel less confident about themselves and their abilities. This behavior results in damaging their already worn self-confidence.

You can be more confident through the total elimination of dependency upon others' judgment. If you don't really have a solid knowledge of your abilities and of who you are, you will most likely be depending on others to tell you who you are and to define your abilities and limitations. If they were satisfied by your actions, then they may tell you that you are a good person; if not, they may label you a fool, an idiot, or anything else that suits their own point of view. You will, of course, welcome these labels and add them to your idea about yourself because you've left the judgment to them from the beginning. Just as your personality affects your behavior, so does your behavior affect your personality. Acting in a non-assertive way results in your feeling less confident and leads to a self-reinforcing cycle. Your continuously decreasing self-confidence makes you even less assertive and this in turn weakens you further. This can also work the other way around, since by forcing yourself to act in a confident and assertive way, you will start feeling more confident that reinforces and strengthens you even more.

OVERCOME YOUR FEARS

Fear is a natural reaction to danger or the threat of injury. If suddenly confronted with a huge dangerous animal, most everyone will turn and run. Likewise, if you are given a choice of doing something you perceive as harmful, you will usually avoid the danger. The problem occurs when the danger is not real or the fears are not rational. Fear can stop you from being successful and can cripple you.

What Can You Do?

> ➤ Analyze the fear. Can it harm you in any way? Confront your fears.

➤ Change the way you think and you change the way you act. You can control your thoughts. Since you're only able to consciously think about one thing at a time, only allow positive thoughts to go through your mind. Whenever a negative thought or fear enters, simply choose to stop it right in its tracks and immediately change that thought to something positive.

➤ Deliberately try to program right thoughts into your head every single day. This is the best way to change the picture of fear into one of victory.

➤ Realize the best defense from fear is a good offense. What you imagine is almost always worse than the truth. So many times the "truth" you see in your mind is only the truth as you believe it to be. So sometimes the best thing is the very thing you fear, even if you have to do it being afraid.

➤ Check your daily mood log. Write down the negative thoughts that make you feel anxious or frightened. Identify the cognitive distortions associated with those thoughts, and replace them with realistic and positive thoughts. Instead of worrying and constantly predicting failure and catastrophes, tell yourself that things will turn out reasonably well.

➤ Substitute reassuring and peaceful images for the frightening daydreams and fantasies that make you feel excessively anxious.

OVERCOMING SUICIDAL THOUGHTS

➤ Don't entertain these thoughts to make someone else feel guilty. You may have these thoughts because someone hurt you recently, and you want that person to feel guilty. It won't work; think it through. You won't be around to see how that person grieves or acts after you're dead. It might be a long time before they even find out about you. And even if they got terribly upset on discovering you did away with yourself, you would not be there to see that reaction. Killing yourself isn't the way to get love and attention from others.

➤ Think of the effect your suicide would have on people you care about. For example, if you are a parent, consider what would happen to your children. They would never truly recover. This can be one of the most effective ways of discouraging yourself from suicide. And think about your own parents and siblings, too.

➤ Protect yourself from impulsively acting on your thoughts by putting dangerous objects out of immediate reach. Preferably give pills, weapons, etc., to someone else for safekeeping, but even putting them in a locked or inaccessible place makes it a little harder to act impulsively.

➤ Tell someone else how you are feeling and get appropriate help. You may need to challenge yourself about what's stopping you from getting help. Be prepared for non-professionals to be shocked by what you tell them, and don't expect a "perfect" response—it is always better to make human contact than to stay isolated and alone with your thoughts.

➤ Both alcohol and drugs tend to reduce your inhibitions and make it more likely you could do something you will regret the next day. Check your alcohol/drug consumption and try to cut down. Try not to drink alone or to be alone after drinking.

➤ Depression and suicidal thinking thrive in isolation. Try to minimize time spent alone—take work to the library, ask friends to be with you at vulnerable times, make plans ahead for weekends and other lonelier times, generally work on building your support networks.

➤ Suicidal thinking is the ultimate all-or-nothing thinking habit, and the culmination of other habits of depressed thinking that intensify the depression habit spiral. Learn how to challenge depressed thinking.

➤ Remember to eat regularly, and stick with healthy food. Avoid sugar, which can contribute to mood swings. If you go too long without eating, you will get low blood sugar, which worsens depression.

➤ Engage in exercise such as jogging or calisthenics. Exercise increases the dopamine levels in the brain, and is also a very good way to take your attention off of emotional pain with a healthy dose of some constructive physical pain.

➤ Finally, if you are actively feeling suicidal and cannot control your impulse, please call 911 or your local crisis team. Remember, help is just a phone call away.

Remember to practice these practical strategies and most importantly practice controlling your negative thinking—preventing it from escalating into a catastrophic event. You can be a winner, but you have to try to win that prize of victory. You don't need a Ph.D. in psychology or thousands of hours of therapy to win the battle against negative emotions and to move up to the next level. But you *do* need to learn some basic facts—the ones you are learning from reading this book. You also need an uncomplicated strategy that is easy to use. Finally, you need power.

When you know the facts, have an effective strategy and real power, the odds shift in your favor, and there is a high probability you will win each battle. It's going to be a dogfight, but it's a fight you can win. You have a choice. You can allow negative thinking and depression to rule your life, or you can reestablish command and control over your thoughts and push your mind in a positive direction.

ENDNOTE

1. Josiah P. Allen, "An Overview of Beck's Cognitive Theory of Depression in Contemporary Literature," http://www.personalityresearch.org/papers/allen.html; accessed May 13, 2010.

Chapter 8

Winning the Battle Through Christ

In this chapter I focus primarily on biblical perspective and also how you can bring about positive mind-set change. When I first became born again in Christ, I struggled with negative emotions and adopted a victim's mentality, which led to my suffering and struggle. You may be going through the same battle. You may feel that there is no escape for you. You may wonder why I am including a biblical perspective. I am including it because I am not ashamed of sharing this powerful testimony that changed my life—and can change yours as well.

During the early part of my life, I had much Hindu influence. I sought answers to my problems and questions through the pagan way, as well as practicing cults including rituals. I took great interest in horoscopes and seeking answers, or rather magical solutions, through mediums. However, I did not find relief; and as a matter of fact, I was getting buried under death. Death was indeed surrounding me, and I felt a complete loss. I was going downhill rapidly until the night I met Jesus. As soon as I acknowledged Him in my life and accepted Him as my Savior, Jesus walked into my life immediately and I sensed an inner cleansing that took place through His blood shed on the cross for me—and you.

At the same time, I received glorious peace in my heart and soul. When I looked more deeply into Jesus and His life, I discovered a powerful revelation of Jesus who gave His life for the entire human race— every caste, religion, sect, race, nationality, and color. I soon realized that Jesus is the living Son of God and to reach out to Him isn't as difficult as with other religions because of what they impose upon you. Jesus was and is the only Person to sacrifice His life on the cross for us so that we can be saved and have eternal life. This powerful sacrifice of Himself and His grace is available to all who call upon Him. This was the turning point in my life.

When a person truly becomes a Christian, there is a visible change in his or her life and this was certainly the case with me. I realized the full impact of what Jesus did for me on the cross and I willingly follow Jesus out of love for what He has done for me. This is not a forced conversion as in Islam. And Christians are not saved by works alone but by the blood of Jesus and His abounding grace. An unsaved person can perform good works but the works are of the flesh and are not of God. Rather than doing good works or donating money to charities as an obligation or to make an impression on others, true Christians do these things because they want to sincerely help others—as Jesus did.

Christianity is rooted in history and evidence, and it has a coherent belief structure. This is how I started my journey into discovering the one true and divine God who still lives and who still awaits for all to come to Him and find rest under His wings. He truly forgives our sins and this is another profound aspect of Jesus that touched me so deeply. He filled my wounds with His balm of love. My mind-set started to change and I thank God today that I am victorious in Jesus.

In the previous chapter, we focused on practical strategies from cognitive behavioral techniques, and in this chapter we are going to explore deeper into correcting our negative emotions through God. Let us not forget, though, that cognitive behavior techniques or other practical psychological strategies are God-gifts that you can utilize daily in perfect combination with what is now going to be discussed.

THE BATTLE FOR YOUR MIND

Your mind is a strategic battlefield and many wars are won and lost on this field. Many Christians today are leading lonely, defeated, and victim's lives—they are easily giving in to losing the battle. The stronghold of the mind of humankind is therefore the strategic center of the "war" with the "god of this age," because it is primarily through the mind that he holds his captives in his power, and *through the mind* of those captives he transmits his poison into the mind of others—his plans and schemes for arousing souls to active rebellion against God. *The mind has never been fully delivered from the grip of the enemy.* Shall I put it crudely and say that many people get new hearts, but they keep their old heads!

> *For though we walk in the flesh, we do not war according to the flesh. For the weapons of our warfare are not carnal but mighty in God for pulling down strongholds, casting down arguments and every high thing that exalts itself against the knowledge of God, bringing every thought into captivity to the obedience of Christ* (2 Corinthians 10:3-5 NKJV).

It is important to understand the mechanics behind this battle raging in your mind. The primary purpose of the negative battleground that satan has deceptively created in your mind is to:

- ➤ Defeat you.

- ➤ Destroy you.

- ➤ Kill you.

- ➤ Paralyze you.

- ➤ Make you incompetent.

- ➤ Make you hopeless.

- ➤ Make you indecisive.

- ➤ Make you a slave in his kingdom.

- ➤ Cause mental disorders.

- ➤ Cause low self-esteem and confidence.

- ➤ Make you worthless.

- ➤ Make you a habitual sinner.

- ➤ Make you engage in pornography.

- ➤ Make you use drugs and alcohol.

- ➤ Make you feel guilty.

Once the battle in your mind is lost, you are just a piece of vegetable. You feel useless, and you have no desire to bring about change. You accept lies as reality, and you paint your personality with negativism.

We cannot win back our own minds by our own power. Battles within the mind must be won by surrendering to God. This often involves overcoming our foolish pride and forfeiting our own precious rights on behalf of and for the benefit of others (and, in the long run, of ourselves). By the power of the Holy Spirit, Jesus *can* and *will* fight our internal (and external) battles for us. He will reopen—and keep open—the gates to our minds and consciences so that He effectively can remain in constant communication with us and can instruct us how to aid Him in fighting His important battles within the world.

We read in First Peter 5:10 that, "The God of all grace who called you to His eternal glory in Christ, after you have suffered a little while, will Himself restore you and make you strong, firm and steadfast." The storms that this life brings will be turned around for your good and will bring you to the knowledge of how wide and long and high and deep is the love of Christ (see Eph. 3:18). It is only after you have been in a painful battle and watched as your God defeated all of your problems that you can grow in unwavering trust. Nothing can overcome you when your life is in Christ. He is your power and the force to go on despite the pain you may be experiencing. God is never limited by the impossibility of your situation. You may be facing a serious illness, an addiction, a broken marriage, or financial problems, but you need to know that God is willing and able to take you through your struggle—that you may be anxious for nothing. We are told in Isaiah 26 that God will keep in perfect peace all whose minds are steadfast, because they trust in the One who can do all things.

This battle, then, that begins at the time of our consecration, our accepting Christ Jesus as our Lord and Savior, continues until the end—our death. Of course there is our physical death—when we move from this earthly world into Heaven where we will live eternally with our Father God. But when we accept Jesus, another death also comes—death of our old self. The Bible speaks about this "old self" that we must lay aside:

> For we know that our *old self* was crucified with him so that the body of sin might be done away with, that we should no longer be slaves to sin (Romans 6:6).

You were taught, with regard to your former way of life, to put off your old self, which is being corrupted by its deceitful desires (Ephesians 4:22).

Do not lie to each other, since you have taken off your old self with its practices (Colossians 3:9).

So far as our earthly interests are concerned, we sacrifice them fully—we exchange them for the opportunity of gaining glory, honor, immortality, joint-heirship with the Lord, participation in the divine nature.

"I have been crucified with Christ and I no longer live, but **Christ lives in me**. The life I live in the body, I live by faith in the Son of God, who loved me and gave Himself for me," says apostle Paul in Galatians 2:20. In your position as a Christian your eternal interests are at stake. Do not fear losing eternal life, God is faithful, and with Him you are an overcomer. Ephesians 1:18 (NKJV) reads, "The eyes of your understanding" being "filled with light." Here is the mind illumined by the Spirit. It is the vehicle of light. You see with the mind, you feel with the spirit. David says in Psalm 77:6, "My **spirit** made diligent search." The mind is filled with light from God in the spirit, illuminating the mind. This brings into action the perceptive faculty of the mind, whereby you, the believer, are able to spiritually discern spiritual things.

This is what we speak, not in words taught us by human wisdom but in words taught by the Spirit, expressing spiritual truths in spiritual words (1 Corinthians 2:13).

The various marginal readings of First Corinthians 2:13 show the new mind in use. It is able to discriminate, examine, combine, compare, and explain spiritual things that the "natural" person knows nothing about. You need to continually be aware of the spiritual warfare in your mind and in the spiritual realms where the devil is doing his best to devour you and destroy you. Be on your guard all the time—God is on your side and will give you the power to resist. The Bible says resist the devil and he will flee from you. Make sure you read and meditate on the Word of God daily, renew your mind daily in His likeness, pray and fast, and as the psalmist says, "even though I walk through the valley of shadow of death, I fear no evil. You, Lord, make me lie down in green pastures" (see Ps. 23). Make every effort to have a true and loyal relationship with God, for He will protect and comfort you. You can win every battle!

OVERCOMING SEXUAL SIN

Many Christians suffer from recurring thoughts and images of sexual and lustful things. They are hooked on pornography and they find it difficult to get rid of these unclean thoughts. This sin occupies many minds and even though they are trying to overcome this sin, they fail in each attempt. With the Internet, television, and magazines, pornography is a sin that many men and even some women struggle. Even King David— a man after God's own heart—wrestled with sexual sin. When he saw a beautiful woman named Bathsheba, he was overcome by his own lust. He then went to great lengths to hide his sin. But thanks to a faithful friend and a forgiving God, David found his way home (see 2 Sam. 11:12). And so can you.

"You have heard that it was said to those of old, 'You shall not commit adultery.' But I say to you that whoever looks at a woman to lust for her has already committed adultery with her in his heart" (Matt. 5:27-28 NKJV). Grasp the seriousness of this Bible passage. You have been breaking a commandment of God. You have turned something beautiful (sex), into something ugly, selfish, and damaging. If you are married, then you have been unfaithful to your spouse. If single, you are sinning against the dear person you may one day marry. You have to face the fact and admit your weakness. You have to accept fornication as a sin and set your mind against sin. Without a commitment and desire to live sinless, then stopping yourself from sexual sin cannot be accomplished. Obedience to this Scripture is essential. Commit yourself to be a living sacrifice. Offer yourself before God. Continue to renew your mind on this resolve, so as not to be conformed to this world. *Transform your mind!* Follow Galatians 5:24, "Those who belong to Christ Jesus have crucified the sinful nature with its passions and desires." Bring every thought into captivity of Jesus. When Jesus was tempted, He countered the thought with a better thought from Scripture, and not by blocking the thought (see Matt. 4:1-11). Don't feel guilty about being tempted with bad thoughts. Distract yourself by pondering on God's Word and praying. Make no provision for flesh. In other words, don't leave even one path open to fall back into sexual sin. This is essential. It's time for many Christians to quit trying to stand face to face with sexual sin.

There is a way to prevent these sins. Get rid of the magazines and videos. Get rid of the bad cable channels or get rid of cable television all together. Having the computer in the common room of the house can work part of the time, but it's rarely enough. On dating and engagement, remember "make no provision for the flesh" (Rom. 13:14). On marriage, First Corinthians 7:2, "But, because of sexual immorality, let each man have his own wife, and let each woman have her own husband." Most cases of adultery are because of the lack of attention, affection, and admiration from the other spouse. It's time to put down the weight of sin (see Heb. 12:1). Know what sexual sin is, set your mind against it, live the Christian life, and make no provision for the flesh.

STARTING POINT

We demolish arguments and every pretension that sets itself up against the knowledge of God, and we **take captive every thought to make it obedient to Christ** *(2 Corinthians 10:5).*

Don't underestimate the degree to which the thoughts you accept as truth impact the words and actions that create the world you live in.

I read the following in a Rick Warren (author of *The Purpose Driven Life*) daily devotional:

> The fruit of the Spirit begins in your thought life. The seeds must be planted in your mind: "The way you *think* determines the way you *feel*, and the way you *feel* determines the way you *act*." God characterized man by having a rational mind. Therefore, man is a thinking being. His thoughts may be of a good nature, e.g. thoughts about service, humility, contemplating on divine matters, etc., or they may be of a bad nature, e.g. vain glory, anger, revenge, lust, doubts, etc. Purity of heart requires that a person keeps his thoughts concentrated on good things, as well as avoiding the bad thoughts.[1]

If you don't make an effort to bring every thought under control and most importantly under Christ's control, you will certainly be the right candidate enroll in the University of Adversity. Adversity will become your teacher; every lesson you learn will influence your thinking to a degree that you will get wrapped in negativity. Once your negative mind is fully up and running, it will fill with junk. Remember, filling your mind with junk is similar to eating junk food every day despite your doctor's advice that this can cause various physical health problems. When you start to feed your mind with rubbish thinking, you will soon suffer from junk overload and a complete shut-down of your brain operating system. This will affect your reasoning, judgment, decision-making, and will make you more vulnerable to satan's attacks. You will also slip into a victim mentality pattern of thinking.

The Bible says in Philippians 4:8, "whatever things are true, whatever things are noble, whatever things are just, whatever things are pure, whatever things are lovely, whatever things are of good report, if there is any virtue and if there is anything praiseworthy—meditate on these things." *This Scripture is the formula for a positive mind.* You urgently need to put good things into your mind. What you put into your mind transforms your life for better or worse. What you listen to in the media changes who you are. What you watch on television goes into your mind and stays forever. You must not walk the path of self-destruction by polluting your mind with toxic waste. Each time you dwell on negative thoughts, you plant the seeds of your own destruction, and those thoughts haunt you for the rest of your life. You can change who you are by changing what you say when you talk to your mind. What you say to your mind is your roadmap to the future. Each word takes you to a specific destination. Therefore it is essential that you *renew your mind in Jesus who will create in you a positive outlook filled with joy.*

Every thought needs to be brought into captivity. This means it needs to be captured and brought under control. When an enemy soldier is found on the wrong side of the line, he is immediately apprehended and restrained and eventually either imprisoned or deported. The whole object is to render him incapable of inflicting any kind of hurt or damage on the friendly forces. In the same way, harmful thoughts need to be apprehended and restrained and either expelled from your mind or brought under control. At this point is where most of us are defeated. Our minds are filled with thoughts and ideas that run about, unrestrained, gathering momentum and support, and undermining us from within. Why do we allow that to continue? I really don't know, but we do. Every thought needs to be controlled. Don't let your mind run away with you down the road of lust, bitterness, pride, anger, worry, and unbelief. Bring those thoughts into submission to the obedience of Christ.

GIVE YOURSELF TO GOD

The warfare against self is the greatest battle that was ever fought. The yielding of self, surrendering all to the will of God, requires a struggle; but the soul must submit to God before it can be renewed in holiness. You may be wondering, *"How* am I to make the surrender of myself to God?" You desire to give yourself to Him, but you are weak in moral power, in slavery to doubt, and controlled by the habits of your life of sin. Your promises and resolutions are like ropes of sand. You cannot control your thoughts, your impulses. The knowledge of your broken promises and forfeited pledges weaken your confidence in your own sincerity, and causes you to feel as if God cannot accept you—but you need not despair. Through the right exercise of the will, an entire change can be made in your life. You will have strength from above to hold you steadfast; and thus through constant surrender to God, you will be enabled to live the new life of faith.

A life in Christ is a life of restfulness. There may be no ecstasy of feeling, but there should be an abiding, peaceful trust. When the mind dwells upon self, it is turned away from Christ, the Source of strength and life. Satan is constantly trying to keep the attention diverted from the Savior and thus prevent the union and communion of your soul with Christ. No tears are shed that God does not notice. There is no smile that He does not mark. If you fully believe this, all undue anxieties will be dismissed. Your life will not be so filled with disappointment as now; for everything, whether great or small, will be left in the hands of God.

DESTROY THE STRONGHOLDS

Strongholds is a military term to describe a fort. It is a place where soldiers build up a barrier of protection; a place from which they can launch an attack, while they themselves are protected.

You need to start pulling down the strongholds keeping you captive. Strongholds include fear, tradition, jealousy, rejection, peer group approval, resentment, bitterness, all kinds of phobias—over 100 phobias have been named—and unreasonable fears. Like many people, you may have one or more of those strongholds lurking in you. Many times it comes out in a dream or a nightmare. You may be terrified by it and never quite free from the realization of it. Strongholds are sometimes expressed in physical maladies or are detected in a recurring proneness to sin, about which you may wonder, "I don't know what made me do that." Something in you is programming your behavior.

So what is a spiritual stronghold? It is an area of a person's life that provides shelter and strength to a way of thinking, a viewpoint, a habit, or a lifestyle. Things that live inside the stronghold are very difficult to change or force out. Demons often live in strongholds in people's lives.

The following is a list of a few strongholds that are common to many people: fear, resentment, bitterness, unforgiveness, apathy, unbelief, depression, anxiety, lukewarmness, sinful thoughts, lust, pride, greed, drugs, and alcohol.

A stronghold may fit one of a variety of definitions or descriptions. It may be like an inner child of your past. It may be something in your background; an episode that occurred that you have locked away in the closet of your mind. Although you have locked it away, it is there as an episode, feeding and controlling certain behavior. It is a stronghold.

For some Christians a stronghold manifests itself as worry that comes too easily, because it was programmed into them. Others easily get depressed, discouraged, or willingly accept misery as a permanent part of their lives. The devil is a great entertainer of your mind and your thought life. He will do his utmost to create strongholds in your mind so that you can lead a defeated and miserable life. Our minds have been tainted and perverted through the influence of our former life and the continuing propaganda campaign of the world.

Remember the enemy, satan, can defeat you in your mind strategically—if you don't immediately remove his harmful thoughts from your mind. He will bring a deception into your mind. He will try and make you believe his lies. He will weaken your personality and torment your thoughts. Satan loves depression and mood disorders because these conditions make you more vulnerable to his deception. In depression, you cannot shut down negative thoughts and satan will use your mind and thoughts to influence your emotions.

Another area satan will attack you is by bringing unhealed emotional baggage from the past. As long as you are carrying painful memories that you have not dealt with, then you are also carrying imbedded lies waiting to be activated. He will then attack you with depression, discouragement, fear, false guilt, condemnation, inferiority, pride, and hatred. Satan has a huge arsenal pointed toward your mind, and it is no wonder that many people suffer from nervous breakdowns, mental disorders, and many other diseases of mind. Satan has one hateful goal in mind—to deceive you. He hates people and wants them all destroyed, living lives of torment.

Another area where satan can occupy your mind is making you doubt. We all battle with doubts and sometimes they can be healthy doubts to safeguard us from a particular danger or mishap. However doubt is a powerful weapon that satan has used throughout generations and from the beginning. However, you need to differentiate between factual doubt and emotional doubt. The most common cause of emotional doubts (and perhaps even all types of uncertainty) stems from psychological states such as anxiety or depression and, in particular, different moods that people frequently experience. In fact, in a certain select sense, psychological doubt as a whole might be termed mood-related.

Intellectual doubts flow from a lack knowledge of God's Word, but emotional doubts are often caused by disobedience to the Word of God. By faith in Christ, we enter into a relationship with God. We become His children. However, when we allow sin into our lives, our intimacy with Him is broken. We no longer experience practically the depth, width, breadth, and height of His love. His love for us hasn't changed. We are still His children, but our fellowship with Him has been shattered. That fellowship can only be restored when we confess and repent of our sins. It's only when traveling down the highway of holiness that we have intimacy with God.

Therefore, remember that thoughts are planted like seeds, and the more you think them, the more they grow. The more you give in to satan's lies, the more your mind will be captured. Meditate on the life-giving Word of God, which will help you push aside lies and deception. This will build strongholds of God's thoughts that will cause you success and prosperity in all you do. In every area of your life, replace negative thoughts with God's thoughts. The first stronghold is to bring your thoughts into conformity with Christ's, and the second one is your obedience to His Word.

DESTROY A VICTIM MENTALITY

As stated previously, a victim mentality can take root in your life if you allow your negative emotions to control your mind. In many cases a victim mentality is planted in your mind early on in your life and it gets ingrained into your personality to such an extent that you just can't stop playing excuses. If you were physically, emotionally, or mentally abandoned or rejected, you may have developed a victim consciousness. Victims may turn their relationships into battlefields, as their loving partner is turned into the evil perpetrator who hurts them. A victim mentality can be thought of as a sick addictive cycle of perpetual misery. Because of the increase of evil in a time when evil is called good and good is called evil, we live in societies and an era when there are many victims of satanic attack and oppression. Satan wants to impose a victim mentality upon us because he knows that if we accept it, we are rendered useless and ineffective as Christians and present no threat to him or his domain.

Everyone faces daily choices. We can become victims in our thinking by taking on the victim mentality and live in the misery of defeat and shame—or we can break free from the victim mentality.

Have a look at the following list of symptoms indicating a victim mentality—note that this list is not exhaustive:

> ➤ Do you constantly focus on the past and believe that what went wrong is all your fault?

> ➤ Do you always blame someone else for the way you are or your circumstances?

> ➤ Do you find yourself frequently preoccupied with problems?

> ➤ Do you feel helpless most of the time?

> ➤ Do you often feel as if you have no control over anything in your life?

> ➤ Do you always feel as if you are always being picked on?

> ➤ Do you feel as if you can never do anything right or you can't succeed?

> ➤ Do you frequently self-blame for all the bad things that have happened in your life?

If you are exhibiting any of the above symptoms, then you are treading on the path of self-destruction. The truth is, you need to be able to feel sorry for yourself once in awhile or feel fear. Who doesn't feel this way when dealing with stress? Having these feelings periodically is part of your normal personal growth, especially when you are facing change. You simply do not want to remain in this state. It is important to feel how you do and have compassion for yourself. Yet, if you stay in this state too long, you risk injuring your self-esteem. Unsuccessful people almost always blame someone else for their situation. In any exchange, the words "It's not my fault" usually enters into the conversation. When people continue to have failures, they continue to play the blame game.

Without taking responsibility for your life and its direction, you are giving your power away to the person you are blaming. Does this person care about your life? Is this person going to fix your life? Is this person thinking about you and your situation?

Get Out of the Victim Mentality

> ➣ You need the truth of God's Word to set you free. It is the only thing that will bring the kind of victory that causes you to break free from the bondages of the past. The principles of His Word must become the guiding principles of your life if you are to truly break this bondage.

> ➣ Take complete responsibility for your life and your choices. When choices you make do not happen as desired, you are in control and can determine how to react to the incident. You can make a decision to learn from the situation, grow, expand, interact with loved ones, and hold your faith close to you. You must face the pain and take responsibility.

> ➣ When you find yourself blaming anyone or anything ever again, remind yourself that you only make decisions for your life and you only can correct them. Keep your power, and you can fully manifest this power by trusting in God.

➤ In the process of looking at your wounds and pain, you may come to the conclusion that you have some major forgiveness, bitterness, and resentment to deal with. This has to be dealt with before the bondage can be broken. This is the first part of the process, because you can't begin to walk in the Lord's forgiveness and victory until you have truly forgiven those who have caused you pain, agony, and conflict.

➤ Apply Scriptures into your life, and try to get rid of an unforgiving heart. Mark 11:25-26 says, "And when you stand praying, if you hold anything against anyone, forgive him, so that your Father in heaven may forgive you your sins."

➤ If you hold on to old hurts, disappointments, petty annoyances, betrayals, insensitivity, and anger, you are wasting both your time and your energy. Nursing a perceived hurt can eventually make it into something more—hate and extreme bitterness. Therefore, be open and be ready to forgive as your Father in Heaven has forgiven your sins. When images of the betrayal or hurt flash in your mind, think of Jesus, for example, and start to pray. Don't throw an error or mistake back in the person's face at a later date. Don't use it as ammunition in an argument.

➤ Choice is always present in forgiveness. You do not have to forgive, but there are consequences for unforgiveness. Refusing to forgive by holding on to anger, resentment, or a sense of betrayal can make your own life miserable.

➤ You must take responsibility for your life and it has to start now. No matter who or what may have caused you to fall into a victim mentality, it is your responsibility to get out of it. You've got to quit blaming and feeling sorry for yourself—take responsibility for your life. Nobody else can do that for you.

➤ Taking responsibility will completely eliminate your desire to hold grudges against others. If something bad is happening to you, accept that it is happening because of a decision you made and bring it into submission of Christ. Know that you thought this way because of the information you had at the time.

➤ In order to eliminate the toxicity of a victim mentality, you need to be Kingdom focused. Matthew 6:33 says, "But seek first His kingdom and His righteousness, and all these things will be given to you as well." When you learn to practice self-evaluation and bring your negative mind-set to Christ's captivity, you will change from victim to victor. As you become more Kingdom focused, you will begin to make the right choices that enact the law of sowing and reaping to bring forth God's blessing and deliverance into your life.

Overcoming a victim mentality means knowing the truth—the truth about your status in God's Kingdom—you are a child of God, an heir to the throne. Knowing the truth will set you free.

ENDNOTE

1. http://www.crossroad.to/articles2/2003/1-purpose.htm Spirit led or pupose driven, by by Berit Kjos, November 2003.

Chapter 9

Reject Distortions With God's Power

I really love what Jesus says in John 8:32, "You shall know the truth, and the truth shall set you free." You need to get to grips with the truth. A distorted lie can give you brief comfort or relief, but lies will eventually be exposed. When evaluating your life or a situation, ask yourself, "Is what I am seeing and feeling the truth, the whole truth, and nothing but the truth?" That's the only way you can escape cognitive (thought) distortions. You must know that only the truth will set you free.

As you learn how to deal with your cognitive distortions, be careful that you don't get into an argument with your mind, because it's impossible to win the argument. Arguing is the recipe for frustration and exhaustion. When you argue with the negative internal critic, you have the wrong focus. You are focusing on negative things, and so they expand further into your mind. Psalms 42 and 43 give a good description of the clinical features of depression and provide assurance that depression is both part of normal human experience and understood by God. The psalmist describes the depressed person's mood changes, loss of appetite, grief and mourning, difficulty in planning, and paranoia. The immediate cause is not clear, but may have been due to circumstances, as a result of physical symptoms or spiritual issues. Depressed people often find prayer difficult, so they need friends who will pray for them, encourage them to put their hope in God, and remind them that better times will come.

I found in my own life that I struggled with negative errors in my thinking, and as soon as I focused my thinking pattern to the cross of

Christ, I was filled with amazing love and peace that only flows from Him. His love for you is unconditional and His love does not compromise with any worldly ways. The Bible says, "Be transformed by the renewing of your mind." The Bible recognizes that your mind is the door through which you enter the world of positive change. You renew your life by renewing your mind. To win the battle against depression and anxiety or any other negative mind-set, you need a mind transplant through Christ Jesus; you need a whole new way of thinking so you can get a completely new way of feeling. God gave you a mind, and He expects you to put good things into it. One of the most important things you need to do each day is fill your mind with positive things.

As I wrote in the beginning of this book, I find it very disturbing that many churches around the world do not place emphasis on people suffering from any form of mental disorder. Perhaps this is because churches are not prepared or skilled in handling mental health problems. Remember, if you have symptoms of depression or anxiety, it is important that you seek professional help. At the same time, though, you need to find healing in the Word of God. I found my healing in Jesus. I struggled with depressive and anxiety symptoms for a long time until I came to know Jesus.

In the Bible are examples of depressive-type illnesses. It is likely that the first humans to suffer from depression were Adam and Eve, after they sinned against God. Other examples in Bible of people who probably suffered bouts of depression are Abraham, Job, Jonah, Elijah, King David, and others. For example, in Psalm 38:6 King David says, "I am bowed down and brought very low; all day long I go about mourning." There are references in Bible that depression was brought upon David due to guilt. David, having committed adultery, was depressed until he confessed his sins. First John 1:9 states, "If we confess our sins, he is faithful and just and will forgive us our sins and purify us from all unrighteousness."

It is also difficult to rejoice when you are surrounded with clouds of depression that are raining negative and critical emotions upon you. I certainly found it difficult to rejoice in the Lord initially. When I became more habitual in rejoicing and putting my hope and trust in my living God, my depression started to lift. You need to humble yourself before Almighty God, and you will find relief under His compassion and love.

First Peter 5:6-7 says, "Humble yourselves, therefore, under God's mighty hand, that He may lift you up in due time. Cast all your anxiety on Him because He cares for you."

Remember what Jesus Christ went through for you. Remember what the apostle Paul experienced, yet remained focused on the eternal rather than the temporary. When you maintain faith and keep your focus on God's love and the hope He has given you for eternity, you can weather the storms of life. It can be done.

Galatians 2:20 says, "I have been crucified with Christ and I no longer live, but Christ lives in me. The life I live in the body, I live by faith in the Son of God, who loved me and gave Himself for me." Work on the cause of your depression and not just with the symptoms. Many times people try to deal with the symptoms rather than uprooting the cause that is driving their despair and uncertainty. You need to live your life based on truth and not just on feelings. Choosing to trust truth rather than your feelings may require a lot of faith. Having faith is one of the most important ingredients to combating life's uncertainties. Trusting what God says rather than your feelings is certainly a more realistic approach to life!

I was caught up relying on my feelings. I would pray, but my feelings were so overwhelming that I was unable to find a resolve in my emotions. The moment I started to exercise my faith muscle, I was able to gain the balance in my life. Exercise your faith and step out boldly. Declare war on your negative emotions. Remember, after you have accepted Jesus into your life, you can win battles because the One who lives inside of you is greater than the one who is in the world (see 1 John 4:4).

Some cases of depression are due to chemical imbalance or other biological factors. If this is the case, you need to also consider antidepressant treatment. If you are clinically depressed and have thoughts about ending your life, you need urgent professional help. It's OK to read self-help books and literature on cognitive therapy, but they are not enough. You need an experienced professional who can guide, help, and treat you out of the wilderness of depression so that you can start enjoying your life again. However, I believe that God can heal and bring about balance even in your chemicals. We serve a living, all powerful, all loving God, and there is nothing is impossible for Him. He wants to help you stand firm in the wilderness while you consistently put your hope and faith in Him.

Change Your Inner Dialogue

You need to change the way you think and feel by changing what you say when you talk to your mind. If you want to change the way you feel, you are going to have to change your inner dialogue. You are going to have to talk to your mind in a different manner. Simply getting rid of your negative thoughts does not automatically make you positive. Getting rid of the negative only gets you halfway to where you want to go. You must install positive operating software if you want to reach the next level and become a positive person. It's not enough to stop being negative. *You need to become a positive person.*

Mobilize yourself by following these practical strategies:

- ➤ Don't be alone; force yourself to be with other people who can assist and support you in recovery.

- ➤ Praise; give thanks to God in everything and every situation no matter how tough the situation looks and feels like. There is no situation too big for God.

- ➤ Rely heavily on the Word of God. If you find it difficult to concentrate, you may find it useful to play background worship music or audio Bible. God's love has enough power to take you from where you are to where you want to be.

- ➤ Know that you are not alone in this battle. God is on your side, and He will give you the power to have a consistently positive mind. God's love not only points you in the right direction, it also gives you the power through Jesus and Holy Spirit to make the trip.

- ➤ Learn to beat depression thought by thought. Do not try to resolve all thoughts in one sitting.

The Bible says in Second Corinthians 4:7-10, "But we have this treasure in jars of clay to show that this all-surpassing power is from God and not from us. We are hard pressed on every side, but not crushed; perplexed, but not in despair; persecuted, but not abandoned; struck down, but not destroyed. We always carry around in our body the death of Jesus, so that the life of Jesus may also be revealed in our body." You have to understand that you are not alone in this battle. After you have courageously started the process of nailing your negative thought life onto the cross of Christ, you will find relief from your burdens. It will require your active participation. You cannot, and you must refuse to, live like a victim. You have to understand the two voices in your mind. The first voice is your mind talking to you about everything that has been stored in its memory bank, all the junk thoughts, all the negative thoughts are poured out into the streams of your consciousness. The second voice is you talking back to your mind. This voice has the power to change the state of your mind bank and push your negative thinking out and replace it with firm and rational thinking.

The Bible says God has given us a sound mind, power, and love— and not the spirit of fear or anxieties (see 2 Tim. 1:7). You don't have to wait for years to make your life better. You can do it today by telling Jesus your story and asking Him to intervene by reinforcing your mind with positive things. What you say when you talk to yourself changes who you are right now, and it guarantees your future will be different from your past. Not only will it be different, it will be better if you put positive things and Christ-like thinking into your mind.

With God you can achieve anything. However, for me, one of the most important gifts in Christ was and has always been the peace from Him I received that surpasses all human understanding (see Phil. 4:7). Every problem has a silver lining, and when I solve the problem, I get to keep the silver lining. The more problems I solve, the richer I become.

GET RID OF GUILT

Punishing yourself with guilt will not atone for your mistakes. If you want to make up for the things you have done wrong, do something positive and strategize to help those who are in need. Don't waste your time and energy in a masochistic guilt ritual. It won't make the world around you a better place, and it won't make your life better or fix the problem that caused the guilt in the first place. Guilt has the wrong focus, and if you continue to live under guilt's power, it will suck up all your remaining battery life. Guilt focuses on your weaknesses and your past undesirable behavior. Guilt can initiate a downward spiral of low self-esteem, undesirable behavior, more guilt, lower self-esteem, and worse behavior. This downward spiral ends in despair, depression, and desperation. Guilty people need love, and they need power to overcome the problem that caused their guilt in the first place. They need to experience the power of God's love so it can wash the guilt from their minds and heal their damaged emotions.

Nothing is more effective at eradicating guilt and transforming lives in a positive direction when you accept Jesus into your life. God loves and accepts you as you are no matter what you have done, but He loves you too much to let you stay that way. Nothing is too hard for God's love. He is the Great Physician and healing broken hearts is His specialty.

THE ULTIMATE CURE

God's love through Jesus is the ultimate cure for your negative thinking and depression. God's love is ultimate, unconditional, powerful, and transforms your life and thinking. When your mind and heart is in control by His love and you have done your part to maintain that balance in your life, you will see that sea of depression, negative thoughts, anxious thoughts, fear, worries, and any other mental symptoms you may have start to lift and evaporate. God designed your mind so that your thoughts create your emotions, and that's why cognitive therapy is so effective. You can thank God for cognitive therapy and the fact that physicians now have a tool that can alleviate depression.

Unfortunately, many psychiatrists, psychologists, and physicians can only provide you with expert opinion on how to deal with your twisted thought life and they may use medication or compulsory detention to safeguard you, but may not be able to help you to go to a different level altogether. They don't feel comfortable telling you what you really need is to become a new person with an entirely new way of thinking, feeling, and living.

And what you need most of all is to connect with the most powerful Force in the universe, God's love. Nothing is more powerful than God's love. When all else fails, when the hand of flesh falls limp, God's love remains unfettered and unstoppable. When His love comes in the front door, misery, despair, and depression head for the emergency exits.

When all therapies and treatments have fallen by the wayside, God's love endures. His love for you will never give up or surrender. There is nothing too difficult for God to do in your life. He is Creator of human mind and heart and He knows where things can go wrong. He knows your limitations. He doesn't need to do any research or seek someone else's advice. God already has the cure for what ails you. He is the powerhouse of unconditional love and has an endless supply that will restore health to your heart and mind. Real power is available 24 hours a day, seven days a week. All you need to do is max out on His love.

Remember, bad things will continue to happen. You need to learn how to strategize to change bad things into new opportunities, and most importantly you need to remind yourself that the victory prize is awaiting your collection. You need to be sharp and active to analyze the whole situation and prepare your counter attack. You need to stay alert and most importantly start spending more time in fellowship with Jesus and the Holy Spirit who will empower you further to face the bad situation like a soldier on duty. If God is with you who can be against you—no one. Start positive self-affirmation in Jesus and upon your mind, and say that you are not going to give in to the situation—you will defend yourself and your circumstances by utilizing the full armor of God.

Many Christians wear the armor of God only on Sundays, and they are quick to take their armor off as soon as they are back in the world. This is where defeats will start to sink into their lives. In desperation they turn to their local pastor or friends to pray for them. They don't realize that they are not far from praying to God. Although it is good to ask to be prayed for in agreement, it is also true that God can speak to us or into your circumstances directly.

You also have the power and authority to interact with God. Your biggest opportunities come when you are willing to do jobs other people are unwilling to do, and you solve problems other people can't or don't want to solve. That is your challenge. Go on the offensive. Look for problems you can attack and solve. If you learn to transform the bad into the beautiful, you will become independently healthy and wealthy, and you will sail on the ocean of your dreams. You have the power and authority to win every battle surrounding you from all directions. Get on the offensive with negative attitudes and thoughts, and make your life beautiful in Christ Jesus.

THE BIG 8

Let us now focus on what the Bible says in Philippians 4:8, "Whatever is true, whatever is noble, whatever is right, whatever is pure, whatever is lovely, whatever is excellent, whatever is admirable, whatever is worthy of praise, think on these things." These eight guidelines should be strictly adhered to in order to receive complete victory in this 21st-century toxic wasteland that influences our minds.

Think on these things, whatever is:

- > True: It goes without saying that the whole truth and nothing but the truth will set you free. There is no such thing as a half truth or misrepresentation of truth.

- > Noble: This elevates people, lifting them up to a higher level.

- > Right: You need to bring into focus the right things that can bring about change in your life. Be spot-on with this.

- > Pure: Purity is where many have battles in their minds. The toxic waste of 21st-century filth is polluting minds. People are focused on "sex, drugs, and rock and roll." You need to remove the junk-thinking pattern from your mind and change it to pure thoughts. This will certainly require perseverance.

- > Lovely: These are the loving things to think, say, and do. It fills your heart and mind with God's love and love for other people. When your heart and mind are full of love, they are exactly the way God meant for them to be.

- > Excellent: Constantly strive to push your mind toward excellence without compromising.

- > Admirable: When you stand back and look at something positive and constructive you have done, it causes a sense of admiration to well-up inside your heart and mind.

- > Worthy of Praise: When you have achieved a victory in your mind, it is worthy of praises. You can now encourage others.

No More Worry

This is another area where many Christians struggle. They just cannot stop worrying over same issue or over many different things relentlessly. They are completely consumed in anxiety and panic states, and some people go on to develop real phobias. People spend lot of money and time trying to find a cure for their anxieties. They engage in drugs and alcohol, turn to the refrigerator, have sex, mindlessly repeat mantras, and escape to cabins, boats, or motor homes to escape from anxiety.

Before you do anything else, reflect on your list of worries. Take a good look through the current events of your life. What is it that has you anxious? Overcoming those anxious fears won't be as easy as simply sitting in a church service or finding some special Bible verse. You probably know that. The truth is, no matter what you are facing, worrying will do you more harm than good.

Internally, we all desperately need the peace of God in our lives. Philippians 4:6 reminds us not to be anxious, "Do not be anxious about anything, but in everything, by prayer and petition, with thanksgiving, present your requests to God." Focus on prayer and thanksgiving, and bring yourself in tune with the Holy Spirit—ask God to bring peace into your life. The Bible is full of promises for you to claim, and you can claim healing.

Jesus was very clear when He talked about anxiety and irrational fears. He instructs us that if we remain Kingdom focused and seek His righteousness, He is faithful to deliver us from any bondage (see Matt. 6:26-34). Are you walking in His peace? Or are you weighed down by anxiety, worry, and tension? There's a simple solution: tell God you are sorry for not believing His promises, begin to give Him first place in your life, and then enter into His rest.

If you are anxious and nervous, in most situations you can realize some relief through practical procedures. First, find someone with whom you can discuss your anxieties. All of us do better when we have a caring friend with whom we can share our burdens. In fact, the Bible instructs us to "bear each other's burdens" (Gal. 6:2), and to encourage each other and build each other up. Next, try to identify the culprits in your environment. Make a list of the situations that trigger and maintain anxiety in your life. Perhaps in your marriage or your daily work there are conditions that you can avoid. If you know that certain situations will cause you difficulty, do your best to avoid or change them. Make sure in everything you do or say, make Christ visible in your heart and mind as this will break through any nagging worries when you start to focus on things from above.

DEALING WITH SUICIDAL THOUGHTS

Suicide remains one of the major final outcomes of twisted, distorted cognitions. When some people cannot find solutions to their burning problems or are suffering from serious mental disorders coupled with loneliness and drug abuse, the easy route to end their suffering is to end their lives. In my medical practice, I deal with the risk of suicide on a daily basis with my patients, and I assess them on a regular basis during routine clinical visits. Many times people will initially begin with self-harming behavior when they superficially or deeply cut themselves or take frequent non-fatal overdoses of medication. However, the primary driver behind these actions is a cry for help. I was surprised to learn from one of my patients, though, that they get pleasure from inducing pain to their bodies.

My Journey Through Suicidal Thoughts

I had suicidal thoughts before I accepted Jesus into my life. My family life was breaking down, my father was on the run due to his financial breakdown, and this greatly impacted our family life. I witnessed many arguments, quarrels, and sometimes physical abuse taking place between my parents. This created a fear and timidity in my soul although my childhood was filled with luxury, comfort, and having several servants in the house to do daily chores. I was devoid of love and affection and never had a consistent father figure to have a stable family life. Just prior to my admission into medical college, I was hanging by the thread. My mother during this time stood by us and provided every need with great difficulty.

I was guilt-ridden and felt in my heart that I could not let my family go through such a turbulent time. My thought processes were becoming more rigid, and I started to have thoughts of suicide. My mother remained a strong tower of strength, even though my family took a deep dive into poverty. I would frequently isolate myself and cry, and a sense of insecurity, loneliness, and depression started to empower me. I lost touch with all my friends and remained very fearful. During my lonely time, I would try to pray but had no idea how because there was no comfort, peace, or happiness in my life. I was broken inside and had many sleepless nights.

My suicidal thoughts grew stronger and stronger with each passing moment. I was constantly arguing with my own thoughts and battling with them. I could not handle my thoughts, my life, and my thoughts were telling me that I was a burden. This voice inside of my head kept telling me that I was a failure and that I could never successfully complete my studies—I would bring shame upon my family. I felt that my life was on autopilot and that there was no way out for me. My thoughts were so overwhelming that at one point it led me almost to the brink of committing suicide by jumping off the top floor of the hospital.

My breakthrough came during my first year as a medical student. While in medical college, I was diagnosed with pneumonia and was admitted into a hospital. I was physically very weak, my mental state was now at the brink of shutdown with suicidal thoughts overwhelming. I would lie on my bed thinking about ways to commit suicide. During this time I was also invited to a revival meeting. A voice inside commanded me that evening to attend the revival meeting, so I went. The preacher quoted John 3:3 when Jesus says, "No one can see the kingdom of God unless he is born again." I returned to the hospital ward and was pondering deeply on what had been said during the meeting.

The same night, while I was still battling with my thoughts, I started to cry uncontrollably and simply said, "Jesus, forgive me." I woke up at about 6 A.M. and I felt as if I had loads of energy, my body never felt that way before. I was smiling, and there was immense joy and love pouring out through my heart and changing into tears of joy. I immediately knew that I had been physically healed, and most importantly I had been forgiven. When the doctors came through for the ward checking on patients, I requested them to discharge me. They were unsure about my discharge as I was extremely unwell and infectious due to my chest infection. They requested additional blood investigations and repeated chest X-rays. When the consultant reviewed the reports, he was standing in front of me speechless as everything came back normal. My suicidal thoughts evaporated. I knew that I was a new person; I knew at that very moment that Jesus had embraced me in His unconditional love. I received victory and have never been the same again.

Risk of Suicide

The reasons why someone may feel suicidal are often complex and may be linked to mental health conditions, such as depression. Often there is no single, clear reason why you are thinking about suicide. A run of small problems or bad luck, or simply a gradual build-up of hurt and pressure over time, can wear you down until you begin to have suicidal thoughts. People with serious mental health problems, such as severe depression, bipolar disorder (manic depression), or schizophrenia, particularly when they have recently been discharged from a psychiatric unit, also are at greater risk of suicide. Also people who use illegal drugs or abuse alcohol. Alcohol and drugs affect reasoning, can act as depressants, and can cause someone to lose their inhibitions, which makes them more likely to attempt suicide. Also people who may feel isolated within society. Gay men and lesbians, students, the homeless, immigrants, elderly people, and those in prison are at particular risk. Also people who have experienced traumatic events such as physical or sexual abuse are at greater risk.

No matter who is at a greater risk, one thing is for certain, thoughts about suicide happen in your mind. You do not have a rational or balanced thinking anymore. You are caught up in your distorted thoughts so much that you do not see any other answer to your problems and focus only on death by suicide.

Steps to Overcome Suicidal Thoughts

Start talking back to your mind rather than allowing your mind to tell you what to do. If suicidal thoughts come into your thinking, you need to challenge them. You need to start thinking in terms of why now and what could be other rational explanations to my problems that are leading me to think this way.

> ➤ Write down your thoughts and each thought you write, you need to find alternative solutions. If you practice this, you will find that very soon you will be able to control your thoughts.

➤ Do not use illicit drugs or drink alcohol, which further fuels your suicidal thinking.

➤ Try not to be alone when you are feeling this way. Communicate with a family, friend, or any other person about your feelings. Develop a list of phone numbers of dependable family members or friends whom you can contact in crisis.

➤ If you are seriously feeling very impulsive, contact your doctor or a medical professional. Remember that professional help can help you overcome these thoughts and can help you with specific treatment strategy.

➤ Recognize your triggers and symptoms and when you notice triggers or symptoms that are potential drivers for your possible impulsive action, contact professionals or family for help.

➤ There may be times when, for your own safety and if you are suffering from a serious mental disorder, hospitalization may be an alternative.

Bible Answers

I find that besides common sense, God is the real answer to your suicidal thoughts. God has a great plan for your life—do not turn a deaf ear to God and get blinded by this world. God has created us in His image (see Gen. 1:26-27). He created us for a purpose. God has a specific plan in mind for everyone. God's plan is for life, not death. The Bible teaches that both physical and spiritual death are the result of our sin and disobedience to God, but eternal life is a gift to those who receive it.

Jesus wants you to have an abundant life of blessings. Jesus says in John 10:10, "The thief comes only to steal and kill and destroy; I have come that they may have life, and have it to the full." Your life is very precious to God; and as matter of fact, it belongs to Him. It is never your place to take your life. The solution to despair and hopelessness is not suicide, but faith in God. Psalm 33:18 says, "But the eyes are of the Lord are on those who fear Him, on those whose hope is in His unfailing love." He is our help and our shield. He will be your help in times of despair, rejection, and when contemplating suicide.

Jesus gives you rest in the midst of your problems, and He certainly did in my case. Jesus says in Matthew 11:28, "Come to Me, all you who are weary and burdened, and I will give you rest." He does give rest to your weary heart. Learn to look upon Him when you are feeling like this. Accept Christ's free gift of eternal life and salvation, if you haven't already. You will see that once you start to repent and ask Jesus to forgive you—you will have His peace, love, and joy in abundance. Because of God's salvation through the death of Jesus on the cross, you can have assurance of eternal life with God.

This is a battle for your soul. Satan wants your soul lost for eternity and God wants you to be saved and your soul to live with Him forever. It is up to you which one wins. You have to fight it, you have to turn to God and ask for His help. You have to ask for His forgiveness and for Him to give you life. Satan won't quit once you are a Christian, but then you will not have to fight satan alone. God will stand beside you and help you; and if you persevere, you can rest assured that the final victory will be yours forever.

Block Out Satan

But satan keeps at you, trying to tell you that your life is not worth living. He tries to convince you that the best thing for you is death. He will tell you whatever you want to hear and once you open up more to satan's lie, he will nurture that lie for you and of course he will do that with your help and support to feed into your mind. If you are tired and want rest, then satan will tell you that death will be rest. If you feel pain, he will tell you that death will bring relief from the pain. If you are lonely, he will tell you death will solve that too. They are all lies! Satan desperately wants to separate you from God, so God won't have the pleasure of showing you His love. No matter how bad your life is now, it is nothing compared to what hell is really like. You won't get away from anything by killing yourself. If you think there is nothing worth living for, well what about Christ? What about your children? Your parents? Your friends? I praise God that someday we will all know what it is like to be able to praise God and never have any suffering or worries, but I also praise Him because today through these trials and stresses and sufferings, I can feel His love for me. I can praise God who was willing to come down to earth and experience headaches, worries, and stresses and even face death for me!

You are not a victim; you are sinful for allowing satan to convince you to think about committing suicide. I am not trying to be mean, I am trying to wake you up and push you into or back into Jesus' arms. You can't get the comfort, peace, and help you need until you confess your sins and plead the blood of Jesus and come to Him, with no excuses. It will be worth it. It is also very hard. It is hard to get up and do what you don't feel like doing, but it is part of life and it is part of being a follower of Christ. Like anything else, it becomes easier the more you do it and practice His presence in your life. Satan would like nothing better than for you to kill yourself. Why? When you kill yourself you won't have relationship with God.

If you have issues that you need to deal with, take them to the foot of the cross and let Jesus handle them from you. If you try to deal with them yourself, then you are saying that Christ did not free you. It takes trust to allow God to take those old pains and hurts and not look back at them anymore. It takes denying self also, because you will have to quit being a victim and start being a victor.

We all claim that we don't want to be victims, but that's a lie. We often enjoy being the victim, it gives us an excuse for our actions, "Well you know I was abused when I was young, so…" "I wasn't loved as a child, so I have trouble loving…" "I have always had low self-esteem so I made up for it by doing bad things…" "I have had such a bad life, I just don't want to live anymore…"

Get victory over your mind and your thought life through Jesus who is waiting and willing to help you and embrace you in His unfailing love. Give Him a chance!

Chapter 10

Break Through Self-defeating Behavior

Self-defeating behavior is the idea that sometimes people knowingly do things that will cause them to fail or bring them trouble. Self-defeating behavior can take several forms in your thought life. Some examples of self-defeating behavior (SDB) follow:

➤ Inferiority feelings

➤ Procrastination

➤ Fear of failure

➤ Dependency

➤ Lack of motivation

➤ Withdrawal

➤ Defensiveness

➤ Poor planning

➤ Fear of intimacy

➤ Fear of commitment

➤ Fear of rejection

➤ People pleasing

➤ Feeling of loneliness

- ➤ Losing temper

- ➤ Giving up under pressure

- ➤ Unrealistic mistrust

- ➤ Paranoia

- ➤ Feelings of hatred

- ➤ Boredom

- ➤ Overeating

- ➤ Using drugs and alcohol excessively

This list is just some forms of SDB. If you have identified readily with any of these or similar behavior, please, it's time to come before your Healer Jesus and repent from your sins and cover yourself with His precious blood. Any behavior you engage in that is self-sabotaging, that takes you away from what you want, or that distracts you from your goals, is behavior that is self-defeating. These behaviors zap your vitality, leaving you exhausted and without access to the powerful energy you need to create your best life.

What makes self-defeating behavior so hard to change is that it works. You do feel better—in the short-term. And the prospect of feeling better overrides your concern about consequences. I struggled myself with SDB for many years during my early childhood and sometimes even after I became a born-again Christian. It took some time for God to deal with my SDB after I started to put more focus on Him alone and changing my mind-set. Sometimes change can happen instantly; however, in certain cases, this change can only happen if you continue to depend on God and His holiness rather than depending on your thought life.

To maintain self-defeating behavior patterns, negative techniques are required—and you need to identify them and stop them. If you make a commitment to stop them, you will stand face to face with the fears from which the techniques have helped you run. Once you are face to face with these emotions, you are ready for the battle. Ephesians 6:10-11 says, "Finally, be strong in the Lord and in his mighty power. Put on the full armor of God so that you can take your stand against the devil's schemes." The opportunity will then be yours to free yourself from your SDB. Some examples of negative techniques to watch out for:

- Putting unrealistic expectations on yourself when you know that you cannot achieve them.

- You start a task but know you're not going to finish it.

- You readily agree with people on the surface when actually you do not agree inside.

- You hang on to old, familiar ways of responding because it seems safer.

- You use an "I am" label (as "an alcoholic," for example) and by so doing view yourself as having a condition. Then you use this as a subtle means for shifting the responsibility for what you do onto that condition, or convincing yourself that is what you *are* instead of what you *do*.

- You quickly put people into categories and react toward them as if they are different.

- You quickly convince yourself by building a wall of deception around you and feed into this wall of deception that only colors your ego.

- You break up relationships as a way of not having to build close and lasting ones, but you make it appear that the other person is at fault.

GET OUT OF THE SDB CYCLE

- First and foremost, bring the behavior to your Best Friend and Daddy, Jesus. Ask Him to forgive you and make a conscious effort to release others from the bondage of bitterness.

- Recognize that you have this behavior that is causing significant disruption to your interpersonal relationships and the way it is controlling you.

➤ Once you have recognized this behavior, think of another positive behavior and replace this with positive self-affirmation. You need to bring this to the foot of the cross and plead the blood of Jesus.

➤ Set yourself a goal to conquer SDB. Keep a record of SDB and reflect on what actions you have taken to overcome it and make sure you record your negative and positive emotions.

➤ Monitor your progress or perhaps ask a trusted friend or family to help you monitor your progress. Meet up or chat with a friend or family member who can appraise you in a constructive manner.

➤ Celebrate your success in Jesus!

➤ Most importantly, you need to remember that Christ has given you self-control, patience, endurance, and love.

➤ Read Galatians 5:22-23, and apply the fruits of the Spirit to your life. Make sure you work on one fruit at a time and once you have mastered nurturing and maturing your fruits in Christ, you can have a life full of the Holy Spirit and all good things.

➤ Recognize also that the devil is the father of all lies. He will do his utmost to plant seed of deception in your life and in your mind. His main purpose is to destroy you and your relationship with Christ. The devil is adverse to you. He is your opponent, your enemy, your accuser. His goal is to distort the truth with a view to eliminating it. He will use pressures and pleasures to accomplish his goal. The "walking about" of the devil refers to him roaring to freeze his prey with fear so that he can pounce on and devour it—you. First John 5:4-5 says, "...everyone born of God overcomes the world. This is the victory that has overcome the world, even our faith. Who is it that overcomes the world? Only he who believes that Jesus is the Son of God."

> ➤ Christ brings all the power, authority, and dominion of God wherever He is present. We are the habitation of God, where the fullness of God dwells. Exercise the authority of the Lord Jesus Christ in all of its power, authority, and dominion. It's who we are!

> ➤ You have to stay close to God and develop intimate relationship with Him and His Holy Spirit. Read His Word. Pray always, even if sometimes you don't find straight answers. And allow His thoughts to influence you and your behavior. Allow the Holy Spirit to lead and guide you, and focus on the positive affirmations and promises that God has for you. Don't allow satan to influence you more than God. The Bible says, "Submit yourselves, then, to God. Resist the devil, and he will flee from you" (James 4:7). Satan does not have unlimited power—he is only as powerful as you allow him to be in your life.

GET RID OF YOUR FEAR

Fearful people are emotionally crippled or paralyzed people. Fear invades like a sudden fog, limiting your view and clouding your reasoning. When you become disoriented, can you find your way out? Does fear paralyze you into retreat, or do you know the way to push on? Fearful people simply cannot make a decision; they are paralyzed by the fear of making a wrong choice; they are obsessed with a fear of failure. As a follower of Christ, you need to make a conscious decision to combat your fears. You are free from fear in Christ. Second Timothy 1:7 says, "For God did not give us a spirit of timidity, but a spirit of power, of love and of self-discipline."

You need to start recognizing your fears, what triggers your fears, and what maintains your fears. Identify them one by one. What is it you are most afraid of? Are you worried your business may fail? Are you scared you will never find a special someone, or that you will lose your loved one? Do you have personal worries that occupy your thoughts? Where in your life is fear of failure diverting your focus and preventing your success? Pray, think, and listen. Let God show you the fear, and then discover how to be free from it. As mentioned throughout this book, fear can be a major stumbling block in your thinking.

For complete breakthrough from self-defeating behavior, you need to learn how to disable your fear and cling to the truth. Your past influences your perception of your present. Like looking through a magnifying glass, danger can appear far greater and bigger than it is when you exaggerate it, because you are still trapped in fear from your past. Take the insecurity or hurt of your past and fight to remove its strength from your life and from your relationships. Trauma, loss, and painful circumstances all contribute to your view on reality. Even little events can lead to unconscious self-defeating behavior in your present, and you will project your fear and worries into the present.

As you discover ways that fear is magnified disproportionately in your life, bring it back into proper perspective. You need to match your fears with the Scriptures, and you have to understand that you need to stand firm and strong in your thoughts by active application of God's Word in your life. God's Word provides clear and perfect assurances that can help control your fears. You can find solutions to fear through the Word. Pray about your fears. Allow God to share your fear with you, to lift some of the stress related to the fear, and provide the power through His Spirit to control the fear. The Bible says that fear has "torment," but as you in faith put on the Word of God in your mind and heart, God's love is perfected in you and will deliver you from all fear.

What is the opposite of fear? For the Christian there can be only one answer: *The opposite of fear is trust—trust in God and His unchanging love.* How should you deal with anxiety and fear? *Turn them over to Christ.* Don't deny them—and don't cling to them. Confess them to Christ, and then ask Him to lift them from your shoulders. Stand firm on God's promises and do not give up.

VICTORY IN JESUS

Yes, you can have victory over your mind and over your life. If you allow Jesus to remain in you, and you remain in Jesus, you can conquer anything and have everlasting peace in your heart. No one can steal that peace from you—ever. Get rid of the toxic mental waste that is hindering your progress toward fulfilling your destiny, which is already sealed in

Christ Jesus. Jesus was and is the Great Psychiatrist, Psychologist, Counselor, and Physician. He will help you only if you give Him a chance.

He is willing, but how about you?

You need to decide today that this is going to be your day of victory. Open your heart and mind to the power of God's love so it can give you a completely new way of thinking and feeling. When your heart and mind are full of God's unfailing love, they are exactly the way God meant for them to be in your life. In fact, there is no limit to how good your life can become when God's love fills your heart and mind. Practice God's presence in everything you do or say and practice His presence in your thought life.

When God made the world, He didn't walk away and or turn His back on His creation. God is still alive and at work in His world. Each day, He pours His love into the human heart and reveals to us His Son Jesus. He reminds us that we can have power and authority over our thoughts, which will keep us from self destruction.

Whenever you see love displayed through what Jesus did for you, you see God's hand at work. Focus on God's love, and then pass it on to other people in order to feel His presence and power. A lot of people have a form of religion, going to church, fulfilling church duties, perhaps even being in church leadership, but their lives never change. Others have a religion based on emotions; and when their emotions are down, they feel as if God has forsaken them. These roller-coaster Christians are like traffic lights, when they are in church they have the green signal and they keep going. However, as soon as they meet with adversity or a problem, they change from amber and then eventually to red, and their life becomes stagnant and comes to a standstill.

God wants your whole mind and your heart moving always toward Him. Jesus tells us to, "Love the Lord your God with all your **heart** and with all your **soul** and with all your **mind** and with all your **strength**" (Mark 12:20). You should make a specific decision to be obedient as a love response from a grateful heart for what your Lord and Savior has done for you at the cross.

When we think about Jesus, probably the last thing that we might think about is Him having to cope with mental health issues. But Scripture made it clear that Jesus would have to cope with mental suffering even before He was born: "He was despised and rejected by men, a man of sorrows, and familiar with suffering…" (Isa. 53:3). The word translated sorrows literally means "anguish or grief."[1] So it is clear from Scripture that Jesus' suffering was both physical and profoundly mental suffering. However, Jesus was not defeated in His work and in His ministry; He stood firm and exhibited excellent containment of His mental faculties. He was not considered disabled. There is nothing in Scripture that indicates that He relied on drugs or alcohol to correct a "chemical imbalance." Rather, He learned from His pain and His mental anguish how to keep His emotions under control, "He learned obedience from the things he suffered" (Heb. 5:8).

You need to develop zero tolerance to a negative lifestyle and thinking pattern. You have to initiate this process of receiving healing in Jesus. I can guarantee you that you will not regret your decision of turning your life and your thinking around. Start thinking about God's love in a big way and allow the wind of God's love to blow through your mind. You need to start saving into God's treasury of love. Fill your mind with His Word and presence.

GOD IS LOVE

The Bible says, "God is love." The power and presence of God in the world is love. From the very beginning, God has relentlessly and unconditionally poured His love into every open heart, and He made His love even more visible through His only and beloved Son, Jesus. It is through His grace and love that we are surrounded and find forgiveness of our sins through His blood.

No matter where you are in this life, no matter how terrible things are going right now, His love and forgiveness will be sufficient for you. Wherever you are, you will sink or swim in His ocean of love. Unconditional love comes from God, and no one else can provide you with His unfailing love. It's not in your chromosomes. You can spend lots of money dissecting the human genome, and you will not find a single chromosome that contains even one molecule of unconditional love, as since the beginning we are sinners and we need to recognize this. It just isn't there. The only way to find true, pure love is to have a talk with God, and let Him put it in your heart and your mind. It's a gift, and only He can put it in there.

Trying to live without love is like trying to walk across the Arabian Desert without water. Millions of people die of spiritual thirst because they are unaware of being totally immersed in God's ocean of love. They don't understand that God's love is the most powerful force in the universe, and that there is no limit to how good their life can become when the power of His love rolls through their lives. First Corinthians 1:8-9 says, "He will keep you strong until the end, so that you will be blameless on the day of our Lord Jesus Christ. God, who has called you into fellowship with His Son Jesus Christ our Lord, is faithful." Likewise, Psalm 18:2 says, "The Lord is my rock, my fortress and my deliverer; my God is my rock, in whom I take refuge...."

RAISE AWARENESS, REDUCE STIGMA

It is also important that churches and ministries around the world raise awareness and reduce the stigma surrounding mental disorders. They need to work in collaboration with physicians, mental health organizations, voluntary organizations, and other charitable organizations to equip and empower themselves, and most importantly the suffering not just within their congregations but also to the wider community. Churches need to be more than ritualistic in producing service after service every Sunday, and not just produce theologically trained preachers and pastors—they need to focus on producing a great generation of ministers who are sensitive to human emotions and can help those in distress appropriately. Church leaders also need to understand the significance of medications and other treatment modalities that, of course, can be combined with strong biblical-based answers. I believe more major breakthroughs will be made and more effective and specific medications are available to those who suffer with emotional symptoms. It is sad when the church heaps guilt trips on any of its members who need these medications, or when it tries to talk them out of taking them.

Jesus came to earth as a man and experienced the complete essence of all temptation. He understands our struggles and our sufferings because He struggled and suffered too. The difference is that Jesus overcame them and He has given us the power to do the same. Hebrews 2:18 says,

"For in that He Himself has suffered, being tempted, He is able to aid those who are tempted" (NKJV). You need to take that first step in Christ—start by saying NO to your negative mind-set and embark on a journey of *"I can do everything through Christ who strengthens me."*

BECOME A PRAYER WARRIOR

Prayer is essential to both the Christian life and the well-being of humankind. The Bible says "…they should always pray and not give up" (Luke 18:1). Christians from around the world are invited to join us in our ministry's prayer outreach. We call this the activity of Prayer Warriors. Our weapon is the weapon of prayer. Our enemy is never another human being. Rather, our enemy is always the evil one, satan, the devil. As we decide to obey God and come to the spirit of God, He will guide us to become effective prayer warriors. Without an active prayer life, which is your connection with Jesus and the Holy Spirit, you are going to fail. The Spirit of God can give us the desire and ability to pray, but decision to pray is purely ours. The Holy Spirit can help us and guide us, but decision is ours. We are controlled by our habits. Prayer must become our essential habit.

If you do not have a set time and place for prayer, you may never be able to find time to pray in your busy life. Prayer and the Word are two sides of the same coin. Through the Word, God speaks to us, and prayer is our response to what He has spoken. These two essential ingredients must be kept together. One without the other is incomplete and useless. We can become powerful men and women under God who can influence our great nations in this generation. Remember that faith without prayer is a dead entity. Remember also that God changes His decisions in response to our prayers (see Ps. 106:23). We must never forget that the destiny of our nation depends on our intercession (see Ezek. 22:30). Praying in simple, concrete language is what Jesus instructed us to do when He taught people the Lord's Prayer. That prayer, found in Matthew 6:9-13 (NIV), is only 57 words long in the original Greek and 52 words in English.

In prayer, you can boldly and courageously go onto the battlefield and even though the battle may appear deadly, you know that in prayer you are fighting the spiritual battle with God who has already won the battle for you. Build a strong prayer life around you, around your family, your children, your friends, and virtually everyone. Pray with a burden for others, and expect that God has already answered your prayers.

The work of Christ on the cross makes major transformation possible, and it can set you free from the bondage of sin and negative thinking. Repeat the following truths regularly in your daily prayer life and see the power of God start to manifest in your life:

> Christ was abandoned so that I will never be alone.

> Christ became sin so I can be righteous.

> Christ was punished so I can receive mercy.

> Christ died so I can experience life.

> Christ was cursed so I could be free from the curse.

> Christ was taken captive so I can be free from bondage.

> Christ was falsely charged so I would not be charged.

> Christ was stripped naked so I could be clothed with royal robes.

> Christ was condemned so I will experience no condemnation.

> Christ submitted to death to deliver me from death's power.

> Christ carried my grief so I can have joy unspeakable.

> Christ's body was torn so I can be healed and whole.

> Christ was humiliated and abased so I may be exalted.

> Christ was forsaken by the Father so I can have full access to Him.

You have now come to the end of this book and I want you pray and reclaim what the devil has stolen from you. You are a very precious human being created by God in His image. You need to have the mentality of a winner. Please say this prayer:

Lord Jesus, today I come before You as a sinner, a person who has been leading a defeated life due to my negative thinking.

Today, Jesus, I am making this choice. I repent of my sins and I cover myself with Your precious blood that has cleansing power. Today I am going to nail all my negative emotions, critical thinking, bitterness, revenge, unforgiveness, anger, low self-esteem, low confidence, and every work of my carnal mind onto the cross where my sins have been forgiven. (Pause here for a few minutes and reflect upon your life; tell Jesus what comes to your mind.) Thank You, Jesus, for coming into my life. Thank You, Jesus, for wiping my tears away. Thank You, Jesus, for making me whole. Thank You, Jesus, for giving me the victory. I ask You now to control my mind and my thoughts so that I become more like You. I invite You, Holy Spirit, to come and minister to me and give me wisdom so that I can discern in my spirit what is right or wrong according to Your perfect will. I am a new person as of today, and I am not going to go back—no weapon formed against me is ever going to prosper. In the name of Jesus, I pray, amen.

ENDNOTE

1. "Jesus and Mental Health," http://www.mentalhealthsolution.com/briefbiblearticles/jesusandmentalhealth.html; accessed May 13, 2010

About the Author

Dr. Sanjay Jain is a psychiatrist working in the National Health Service in the United Kingdom. He is a very passionate Christian serious about sharing the good news of Jesus Christ. He has saved many souls for Christ. He lives with his wife, Christina, and their two daughters in Exeter, Devon.

Dr. Sanjay Jain can be contacted via e-mail at:
victor0768@doctors.org.uk

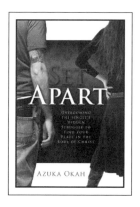

Additional copies of this book and other book
titles from DESTINY IMAGE™ EUROPE
are available at your local bookstore.

We are adding new titles every month!

To view our complete catalog online, visit us at:
www.eurodestinyimage.com

Send a request for a catalog to:

Via Acquacorrente, 6
65123 - Pescara - ITALY
Tel. +39 085 4716623 - Fax +39 085 9431270

"Changing the world, one book at a time."

Are you an author?

Do you have a "today" God-given message?

CONTACT US

We will be happy to review your manuscript
for the possibility of publication:

publisher@eurodestinyimage.com
http://www.eurodestinyimage.com/pages/AuthorsAppForm.htm